Ignition
A Digital Business Development Framework

ANGELO CASAGRANDE

IGNITION FRAMEWORK

Copyright © 2019 Angelo Casagrande

IGNITION FRAMEWORK

CONTENTS

IGNITION FRAMEWORK

INTRODUCTION

This manual pops up in an attempt to rationalize and schematize a (big) handful of guidelines, techniques, mindsets, and methodologies that I've gotten used to dealing with and mixing throughout my ten-year journey in growing the digital agency I founded, and another three years following over sixty startups at various stages: from those who had nothing but a (wacky) idea and struggled even to flesh it out, to those bagging a couple of million in funding, not to mention the dozens in seed-stage.

Having gotten my hands dirty with product development, promotion, and sales in both SMEs and Corporates, and seeing that many startup founders in early stages often come from SMEs and Corporates, I realized that the approach to marketing and sales, especially digital, is still, to this day (I'm writing this at the start of 2019), bogged down by the heavy and frustrating legacy of the '90s. And as much as it's a given that changing the way things work in an SME (and worse, a Corporate) from the bottom up and quickly is tough, the paradox is that in all the startups I've worked with or followed, I found the same archaic thinking and the same resistance to change, especially in their reasoning.

Moreover, I often find it hard to explain to the people in front of me how we're going to work together, why they should start thinking differently, how the execution changes depending on the goals set, or why and in what timeframe my approach "pays off", and especially in what terms it does. Because the truth is, my approach, being set up for rapid learning on the go, always pays off the moment you learn something new and make a new decision, every time you change course even if it's totally wrong. My approach, therefore, always "pays off": you just need to know in what currency you want to be paid.

Over the years, I've also realized that most people aren't inclined towards "trial", Chaos, the lack of reference points: even when they don't have any, I've noticed people prefer clinging to their assumptions and presumptions rather than navigate by sight (and often in the dark). People, even the smartest ones, need systems. Boundaries. More or less defined limits. Boxes, rooms, contexts in which to act. They need security, rules. Rules to break, but rules nonetheless. And, perhaps, despite the chaotic and inconsistent person I always thought I was, I need them too.

Hence the idea and the need to put some order into the array of methods and techniques I use daily for myself and put them into a more or less precise reference system, so as to explain to myself how to act in every context, and so that others can use the same method or build upon it.

The term "digital marketing" can no longer be tied exclusively to "running campaigns on AdWords and having an ever-lower CPC - Cost Per Click". Digital marketing is a set of techniques to be used in a much broader figure: business development. Marketing and sales must support the business goals of the enterprise. And if they tell you that a "growth hacker" will sit down and make you millions using strange software and more or less scientific approaches, they're probably underestimating everything behind the concept of "making millions".

Ignition is a series of rules, methods, mindsets, and techniques to think and execute modern digital marketing and sales. It's adaptable to teams of any size, in any context from startup to corporate, and above all, it's a starting point for any organization that wants to develop its own method on top of it or apply it to its techniques.

1. PROBLEMS OF THE TRADITIONAL APPROACH

1.1 BUDGETING

We've all been there: how much budget to allocate for this year? How much for the semester? How about just for next month?

The first type of response is usually the result of a poor algorithm called "gut decision": it starts from a not-so-obvious assumption, the intended revenue, but the solution takes unpredictably different turns depending on perspectives driven by sentiment. The second, somewhat more analytical, concerns other parameters such as margin, return on investment, or - in the best cases - the history of a previous period (a month, a quarter, a year). Some examples:

a) Applicable from a corporate that allocates budgets

to various departments, to a startup, and even an SME with a general manager or directly the entrepreneur: "we must invoice a million this year, so doing the math quickly we might invest 1% (10k) / 5% (50k) / 10% (100k) of that million." These three cases usually reflect the personality of the decision-maker: miserly (squeezing profits), conservative ("we need to spend them"), courageous (investment). A side note: every time I heard these words, the speaker had never done any real calculations; they only had the distribution of revenue in percentages for each unit of the business in mind. Another side note: a lifetime ago, the first time I wondered how much budget to allocate for marketing/sales, I Googled "how to plan a marketing budget" - the results matched exactly the "1% / 5% / 10% of what you want to invoice" model.

b) Applicable to an SME and a funded startup: "to start with, if we only break even, that's fine." A statement that seems unprejudiced, courageous, and with a vision towards a later time. It seems to postpone further decisions until a first reference point is reached, and it seems to set a short-term goal without too much "over-building", already planning to burn cash (business costs obviously don't just limit to marketing and sales) in exchange for an initial market conquest. Unfortunately, it is rarely like that: normally this solution is a compromise between postponing the moment of important decisions and evaluations of one's performance and still setting at least a minimum economic goal (break-even). Of course, it never accounts for the money burned in disastrously fated attempts, nor how that break-even goal will be operationally reached - that is, which KPIs (Key Performance Indicators) must be achieved to reach that famous break-even. Moreover, in this approach, the break-even is usually calculated monthly or quarterly, and the most common consequences are saying "we are doing poorly" because the break-even was not immediately reached in the first month, then struggling with the business goals of the year, then trying to reach the global break-even in the second month by raising the bar, repeating that we are doing poorly, complaining that "we are not making a margin" when finally we break even for a period.

c) Applicable from the SME to, although it may seem paradoxical, the early-stage startup: "We must have an ROI - Return On Investment - that is at least 110%" - in short, we need to get back the money spent plus 10%. The 10%, depending on the gut of the speaker, can also become 50%, 100%, 200%. The use of the term ROI, in this case, serves to boast of having a good handle on the situation and to give (unfortunately only hypothetically) a clear line to everyone who will then have to pursue the goal, a "rough" growth goal. Following this stance, I have rarely heard anyone question "okay, but how and when do we evaluate the ROI?". The main consequence, on average, is to start making the first sales and say to oneself, "this customer made a 300€ order, but we spent 500€, we should have made at least 330€".

A long time ago, I had a client who sold goods abroad

to points of sale (B2B) - a company with about thirty employees that invoiced just under five million a year. Perishable and consumable goods for the end customer, which means quite recurring purchases by the point of sale. I remember a delirious meeting in which, after four hours of him repeating that our performance was poor - in itself, not compared to other channels since 100% of his customer acquisition now came from the digital, that is from us - he told us that a good ratio would have been to collect from the customer five times the expense to acquire them.

Considering that his customer, excluding some really huge outliers and before even dividing his clientele into different clusters, on average ordered twice a month and that the average order was 300€, considering that historically the average lifecycle of a customer was two years, the LtV (Lifetime Value, the revenue generated by a customer over their entire lifecycle) was 14.4k€. Moreover, considering the sector, 600€ per month of orders from each customer in that case would have been a relatively low value, on which one could have worked during the year to raise it. Our CAC (Customer Acquisition Cost) was about 500€. Our entire setup, which included the total management of digital marketing, consulting and digital support to CRM (Customer Relationship Management), the perpetual development and management of e-commerce (90% of purchases finally went through e-commerce after a relatively short transition period from complete offline) cost less than 20k€/month. Even if we aggregated the entire cost of the "shack" and divided it by the number of monthly acquisitions of new customers, a new customer was costing him about 1.5k€. And, historically, he was producing 14.4k€. Not having further marketing costs on CRM, the repurchases after the third were in fact included in that "acquisition cost".

We first asked him why we should specifically collect "five times the expense", instead of six or ten or two. The answer was "because considering the margin we make - always censored to us - it is a good value." The business goals were not shared with us: it was up to us only to take absurd orders and try to realize them completely in the dark.

We then pointed out that even aggregating our entire cost (not exclusively dedicated to acquisition, which represented about 10-20% of the work) the LtV of 14.4k€ was 9.6 times the acquisition expense. The answer was that this was not a calculation to be made, and that we had to collect five times as much as the acquisition expense right from the first order - as a bonus on the aggregate of our work. This, doing the math, could only happen in two situations:

a) each new customer should have cost a maximum of 120€ (almost a fifth of the current cost, almost a tenth of the aggregated cost of our contract) - impossible;

b) even lowering the acquisition cost, each new customer would have had to produce orders at least two or three times higher than the historical average of the customer;

c) in any case, even lowering the CAC and raising the order volumes from the first (two parameters that do not agree because raising the volume of the first order creates a higher barrier to entry and therefore increases the CAC) this assumption would have meant, at the hypothetical rate of fifteen new customers per month, a growth of 1.17 million in a year (over 20% of its turnover) carried out with about 35k€ in a year (about 3% of the expense for about half of the work). Totally nonsensical? Perhaps.

d) the most flawed case in the world, generally applicable to corporates: budget allocated in January, sales targets set, the team receives it, plans it with the aim of spending it all, spends half the year planning activities to allocate the budget for the following year. The most common consequence: by June there is no longer any budget to experiment with anything, nor is there much concern, because the goals are achievable and all long-term.

e) The case that is theoretically more foresighted, often observable in "funded" startups, typically tries to rely on an "algebraic" approach where there is actually very little science involved: "Acquiring a new customer is costing us 150€, as a business goal we've set to acquire 250 this year, if we reduce the CAC to 100€ we need to allocate 2k€ per month." This case seems to make perfect sense, were it not for the fact that it mixes two long-term objectives (increasing customer acquisition volume and decreasing acquisition cost) that are in conflict. Even just increasing the acquisition volume is not linear: if we're on a pace of ten new customers a month, increasing the pace to twenty doesn't mean "spending double," due to a huge set of variables. To cite one, the acquisition volume (quantity over time) depends closely on the audience being "ground through": if my potential audience is 50k recipients, and in less than a month I cover all of them more than three times (regardless of the channel I use), to increase the monthly volume I only have two ways: try to raise the CR (Conversion Rate, the rate of conversion to a goal, for example, "sale": if one out of every hundred visitors makes a purchase, my CR is 1%), and in that case, if I succeed, with the same budget I will bring in more customers, thus spending less, or try to further insist on the same audience transversally on different channels, with more messages, using longer funnels. This means making a greater effort to convert the user I haven't already converted at the first attempt, and therefore implies a higher CAC (with the same CR) on those particular customers, thus a greater expense than just "double" to increase the volume. Unless I manage, at the same time, to increase the CR, which I will probably not be able to double, so with little likelihood, I will be able to maintain the required performance while staying within the allocated budget.

The consequence of this reasoning often falls into

two categories: denial ("it's not true/I don't believe it, let's just do it") or a compromise ("then let's do 15 instead of 20 and 150€ instead of 100€"). Both fail to consider the real needs and clear business goals in the long, medium, and short term.

In all these examples, marketing and sales budgets are generally calculated and allocated separately. We'll return to the eternal struggle between marketing and sales later, but the main point on budgeting, in my opinion, is to take into account all historical metrics and KPIs, both marketing and sales, and the technical factors of each that either facilitate or complicate the achievement of new business goals, to adjust the budget or, conversely, the business plan, treating marketing and sales as a single entity that supports each other.

1.2 MARKETING/BUSINESS CORRELATION

Digital marketing often seems like an end in itself: a series of tools and techniques that are used to either increase volumes or somehow try to reduce costs.

Instead, digital marketing, just like sales, should support business development (which is not necessarily and exclusively about "revenue growth") and thus the achievement of certain business goals of the enterprise. In my experience, I have encountered several particular cases where marketing was treated as a practice unto itself.

a) A funded startup operating in the restaurant industry. At our first evaluation meeting, their main business development KPI was customer acquisition (restaurants or bars without kitchens). During the meeting, I found out they were perfectly in line with their business plan (a rare event in this environment) thanks to a massive deployment of sales efforts. I discovered that sales performance was actually very high, albeit costly, which was not too relevant at that time, since the objective was to reach the first five hundred served clients - market penetration - and achieve 300k€/month in MRR (Monthly Recurring Revenue): on average, sales closed 50% of the clients they engaged.

Meanwhile, on the marketing side, they struggled to spend a meager budget of 1k€/month and brought in about 8 leads per month, with no track of how many were converted into customers. I wondered about this huge gap, and upon examining their website, the main error arrogantly presented itself to me: everything that was pitched to me by the co-founder in charge of sales was not reflected in any of the marketing mediums. In fact, despite a clear initial introduction, it was hard to understand what they did when I limited myself to reading their website, their emails, and their ads.

I raised this issue with their marketing manager, leading to an aberrant discussion that, after touching on major '90s clichés such as "brand value" and the excessive use of the word "awareness," I tried to cut short by asking why, if his reasoning was impeccable, his performance was so inferior compared to sales. His response can be summarized in a single concept: according to him, marketing cannot be equated with sales because it simply "must use different and creative values and narratives compared to what salespeople use."

In this specific case, repeatedly patched and contained in some way, while salespeople were left with the task of getting their hands dirty in the field and generating revenue, marketing was treated as a creative game where the most disparate arguments were narrated to "stand out" and "be cooler." Performance was still (inexplicably) calculated in terms of leads and converted customers, to the point of declaring a problem in being able to spend the budget beyond the poor contribution to the business goals of volume and revenue, goals that were however sacrificed in favor of a creative narrative and marketing tools that followed the guideline of "we do it this way because it's cool."

My first intervention, in this case, was to copy verbatim the salespeople's storytelling, updating it based on their feedback (no one inside knew the clients, their resistances, and their objections better than those who went out every day to talk to them) and replicate it in all digital tools. The result was, from the first month, an increase from eight to fifty monthly generated leads, stabilizing the overall conversion rate (both physical and digital) from free trial to generated account at 45% (the offline performance alone was at 50%), and achieving a digital incidence on the number of generated clients around 35% (over a third of every 100 clients generated came from digital).

This approach was the first step in, later, changing the way marketing and sales operated: from distinct to a single entity, with a single budget and globally calculated costs. For a single, small, but fundamental reason: if a salesperson physically cannot increase the pace of acquisition on the street because their time is limited and the efforts in processing the client are enormous, if digital on one side converts part of the clients automatically and on the other side provides sales with already informed, processed, and educated prospects, the time sales need to close a first sale decreases drastically, increasing acquisition volumes and reducing their costs.

b) A seed-stage startup operating in the B2B or B2C sales sector, initially providing its clients with a "virtual" sales network made up of multi-mandate sales agents, as per their vision. The case was emblematic for assessing the role of marketing at a stage where the company and its processes were still being defined. At the first evaluation meeting, the company was presented as having no issues, at most a single problem in the volume of acquiring sales agents to then resell to clients. I discovered that almost nothing had been done since the company's inception in this regard (just some email marketing and phone stalking), also because there was no one on the team with any relevant expertise, and I began to test firsthand what channels and methods could be used to engage. The "official" multi-mandate sales agents are difficult to contact through traditional channels, but I managed to find a solution using a mix of AdWords (keywords related to multi-mandate contracts search), Facebook (audience of sales agents, very narrow but with some public), LinkedIn used in a semi-automatic and "creative" way. I quickly realized that the cost of an enrolled agent was exorbitant compared to the business plan, and most of those registered on the platform either did not apply to receive the sales mandates offered, or received the mandate but then did not sell.

Upon rapidly studying the sales history, I realized that the best sellers were not really multi-mandate sales agents, but "business finders". People who in their lives do another job, often related to sales but not necessarily, and who use the platform to round up using contacts or other networks already in their possession, without too much effort and without producing large volumes of sales. Moreover, I noticed that a barrier to entry for applications to mandates was due to the fact that "training" on the product for potential agents was organized and managed through real-time webinars. This meant a ton of operations to manually contact all registered agents, find one or more dates that match their availability and that of the client, only to cancel the webinar three-quarters of the time due to organizational problems, thus permanently losing the agent who, being a multi-mandate agent, already has little time and then had it wasted.

The "marketing" (in quotes because I still don't truly see it as marketing, especially in this case) here played a fundamental role, agnostic to the "given task" (finding new multi-mandate sales agents within a certain cost): in four weeks, identifying the main obstacles in the rapid development of the business. Because the point should never have been "recruit more multi-mandate agents while maintaining a given cost," but rather "generate more sales for clients". And the first action to be taken, given the data and its interpretation, should have been twofold:

a) Eliminate the training via webinar and forget it forever. My suggestion was to try something much simpler: a PDF with all the information on the product, the clients, and how to sell it. If it had gone poorly (in terms of applications for the mandate and sales production), the next step would have been to try something increasingly complex. But it already worked with just this simple action. In this case, the "marketing" had greatly reduced operational times and efforts, unlocking the two main KPIs: applications and sales.

b) Change the source: if the goal was to develop sales for clients and the best sellers were people who had nothing to do with "multi-mandate sales agents," replicating the acquisition on profiles similar to those who were already producing the majority of sales would, in theory, lead to a significant reduction in CAC (improperly in this case, the cost of user acquisition), an increase in the conversion rate (registered users over engaged users), and therefore a good increase in the volume of agent acquisition.

The next step would have been to determine how many "agents" were needed to produce how many sales for how many clients, in order to identify and divide the potential audience into clusters and begin to define acquisition budgets based on the actual performance generated for the client. This would then allow for the definition of the entire budget for the acquisition system and CRM based on the Lifetime Value (LtV) of each client (being a revenue-share model, not too difficult to calculate).

However, I didn't get that far. Despite the data, the business goals were not modified, and there was too much resistance to changing the model and source (my job suddenly became "running campaigns to recruit agents at an ever-lower cost regardless," without correlation to other reference points or specific business goals), so I decided to step back.

Months later, the startup was finally working on a model more similar to "Uber Pop," and no longer on a revenue share but on a pay-per-lead basis. Offline lead generation, in other words.

The moral of this second case, beyond the speed with which changes in direction and modifications to business goals can be undertaken, is that this is a typical example of why the topic is not "marketing" or "digital marketing," but business development, understood as a global concept, including changes to processes and products.

1.3 THE DYSTOPIA OF "MUCH/LITTLE"

Entrepreneurs and teams often compare values that are not shared. "Much/little," "good/bad," "a bit," for example, are just adjectives and as such are entirely subjective and variable depending on the different contexts in which they are expressed. An "eight" might be "good" on a scale of one to ten, but could be "horrible" on a scale of one to a hundred. And it's not even true: a "seven" might not be good on a scale of one to ten when the goal - already achieved in the past, perhaps - was "nine," just as a "ten" on a scale of one to a hundred could still be a good result if the history was close to "zero" and the goal was "to at least reach eight." If I write the numbers in letters it's not literary delirium, but because I've noticed that it has become all too fashionable to hide behind the use of numbers to give a scientific imprint to one's arguments, while numbers in business development should be used as "indicators," thus devoid of value if not contextualized in a system chosen a priori (and then, perhaps, modified). Some examples:

a) Early-stage startup: "We are doing quite well, in the end, the last few months we were doing about 4k, this month we did 5k." They had been up and running for a year. With a B2C e-commerce in the food sector. I wished someone would bury me alive. In what universe, with large competitors making big money, is going from 4k to 5k after months a good result? "Well, it's over 20%

more." Even 1.22€ is over 20% more than 1€. Would they have celebrated the same way? Probably not.

b) SME between 5-7 million in turnover: "This year is going very badly, we will probably close with about a million less than last year, your work is useless." Digging into the data of the subject in question (which we had access to as we had to deal with it by force, otherwise we would have been censored for years), we found that the previous year they had about 400 clients after fifteen years of activity. Of these, about 30% were producing excessively less than 1k€ of MRR, 30% were average at 1k€ of MRR, almost 20% were above but close to 2k€ of MRR, almost 20% were making a leap above 100k€/month (they were a different type of client) and in all this sea there were two outliers making one million a year each, two million a year the other. Checking the current year's data, the million customer (present for about ten years) was no longer ordering, while the two million customer had produced half the expected amount (500k€) by mid-year. However, in projection, we would close the year just under 500 clients, with the clusters seeming to hold (about 35% were on the 2k€ MRR band). After asking a couple of questions, it turned out that our client had quarreled with his million customer, and that the two million one simply wasn't selling as much as before and had started to produce monthly orders exactly half of his historical standard. Essentially, our client had entrusted half (or more) of his business to two monstrous outliers who were very loyal to him and had never grown over the years. Nonetheless, by acquiring handfuls of smaller new clients (including by mistake a couple from the higher band, already outliers themselves), we managed to compensate for what could have been a loss that would really, really hurt. But we were the ones saying this, as we had the task of bringing growth and had as a reference system huge growth, while the client's reference system was turnover, regardless of which clients died and how much his most loyal clients ordered.

The real problem here wasn't defining who was right. The problem was at the root: our client refused to work towards objectives, and we reveled in that context because without long-term objectives there can be no short-term ones and any discussion would be resolved by "massaging the numbers" and showing some kind of rapid growth using the combinations of metrics that pleased us the most. Growth, moreover, that we achieved blindly never agreeing on precise objectives with the client. Every conflictual situation ended in a stalemate where we were both insulted and praised by someone on the client's team, while we returned the accusations to the sender and proposed to give us objectives that were consistently refused by the client. In the meantime, invoices were (almost) regularly paid (also because the goodness of our work was recognized), so as a result a situation full of opportunities to work on every time revealed itself as a stagnant business of which no one was able to say whether it was going well or badly, nor was anyone incentivized to stir the waters by taking the risk.

c) Funded startup. "It's not going very well: yes, we have acquired more clients, but we are spending a bit too much compared to the ROI." The goal in that case was to forcefully enter the market and quickly become a recognized player in the sector, however small compared to the giant competitors. Objectives in terms of acquired clients and turnover had been set, and both had been met during the year, moreover as per the business plan. But the sentiment of one of the founders, completely out of the evaluation scheme, was negative. I asked how much the ROI should have been, he replied that he had only sketched it out as an idea but that it had never been a KPI because it was not a goal to be achieved. I asked how much they should have spent, seeing as they were spending "a bit too much", to answer he read the CAC metric and lowered it by 50%. I pointed out that lowering the CAC by 50% would be a very long job that included technique both in advertising distribution and in marketing tool and automation work, which would anyway by definition lower, along the process, the volume of monthly acquired clients, and that if he wanted we could set it as a macro objective for the following year and build the strategy in blocks to achieve it. He replied that the following year we certainly couldn't stop but had to increase volumes, and in the meantime, we talked about how much the sales department was costing, which was completely on another solar system compared to the marketing one, but that was not a problem because the goal remained market expansion, and if ever turnover (something more easily achievable by acquiring clients with higher LtV and

MRR generated, thus with higher acquisition cost and decrease in volumes). We only came out of it by telling ourselves that "we would work on the objectives while still keeping some kind of eye on costs" - a phrase more or less empty of meaning.

d) Funded startup. "I have put the new site into production, I have decided to do it this way and that because I think it converts more." They had already changed the site twice in a few months (another situation that, especially in startups, seems a constant). With very different trends, but from each experiment in the end, clear signals emerged of what worked and what absolutely did not. The site put into production violated every single guideline learned and built in the last semester, and communicated features of the service that even the rest of the team struggled to understand. Moreover, the CR, at the end of the semester-long process, had gone from a meager 0.3% to a more decent 1.1%. I asked "converts how much more?" - the answer was that he didn't know, he would have to see the data of how much it converted before. Actually, in this anecdote, I made a merge of three different cases, each interesting for its absurdity. The "funny" part is that probably all three (or even those I didn't include in the merge) will find themselves in the same case as I've told it. And this, more than anything else, means that you must stop using evaluations like "much/little/good/bad" and "more/less" to justify your actions decided exclusively based on how much your stomach hurt that afternoon.

1.4 LONG TERM VS. SHORT TERM

There exists a perennial and enormous fracture, never healed, between long-term planning and short-term planning. Long-term strategies require a lot of planning based almost entirely on a bunch of untested assumptions, while short-term strategies, by their nature, require much less planning, bring results extremely quickly, are much more controllable and reprogrammable with less effort, and have a higher probability of success. Like almost everyone from my generation (and the ones before), I was born into the legacy of "waterfall" management, with five-year cash flow business plans, with very long-term strategies based on purely hypothetical objectives and evanescent KPIs. Having had to deal with my own enterprise, and having started doing digital business just under a year before the 2008 economic crisis, a period during which I encountered a disproportionate number of "old school" characters and of which I saw the corpses floating down the river in the following two or three years, I had to learn to change my way of thinking (even if immature, already full of axioms dictated by the aforementioned corpses) and approach to business and product development - both mine and my clients' - and for years, following the principles of Agile development and the Lean Startup, I became a fanatic of the chaotic short-term approach, of improvising, of not wasting time planning because plans never go as you had imagined them.

Then, however, I had the opportunity to meet people from the "new school" who were very, very bright, to deal firsthand with their experiences, to have been able to take further long steps once my business venture was (almost well, by the way) over, and to have been able to do it at a somewhat more mature age and with a baggage of experiences behind me that allowed me to evaluate what I saw in a totally different light. And I learned the downsides of the "hic et nunc" approach: short-term strategies indeed bring immediate results, but immediate results lead nowhere if you don't know where you're going or where you want to go. The short term does not allow space for reasoning, while the long term (still fragmented into cycles suitable for the speed of the world we live in) allows you to decide where you want to go at every point, guided by a preliminary vision that, as much as it can - must! - change over time, still imposes a direction, a hypothetical point of arrival around which to focus one's efforts and actions. Short-term strategies do not allow for the vision, analysis, and sophistries necessary in life to interpret the "big picture."

Thanks to my new, recent, and condensed experience, I have learned that not only should there not be a dichotomy between short and long term, but that, having tried them on my own skin in work and especially in everyday life, hybrid strategies offer the best of both approaches, are more controllable, and offer much more space for discussion and growth (therefore, when talking about business, for development). There are not necessarily specific mistakes in a short-term or long-term approach, simply one does not exclude the other and, indeed, one should be contained within the other.

In addition to treating marketing and sales as a single entity, another pillar of this framework is having a method to plan in the long term but act in the short term, modifying the "masterplan" according to the feedback we receive from the market as we go along. I will delve deeper into the technical section on how to apply hybrid planning between long, medium, and short term to digital business development in this precise order of dependency, and how to use the short term to modify the plan in the medium term and achieve goals in the long term.

1.5 OVERCOMING THE CONCEPT OF "MARKETING" WITH DIGITAL BUSINESS DEVELOPMENT

Startups and companies often misinterpret the concept of "digital marketing," likely deviated by the legacies of traditional marketing. In the best-case scenario, they see it as a mere tool to produce a few extra sales, in the worst as a means to do "awareness" at reduced costs. However, business development isn't exclusively about sales. Or rather, growing a business implies a myriad of additional concepts and phases, as well as variables and shaky balances to be achieved during growth. More than half of the practices used in digital marketing should not aim directly at a sale, but at pushing necessary business metrics, boosting KPIs, automating processes entrusted to humans (speeding up times and reducing costs), and providing strong feedback and guidelines for product development. Generating revenue within a certain time and with specific costs should be the natural consequence of excellent mixed execution between marketing, sales, product development, and operations.

Furthermore, startups and businesses tend to always keep marketing separate from sales. Two different entities that work towards a common goal unknowingly, without talking to each other or sharing the goal. Some focus on the short term, others on the long term, blaming each other: salespeople blame marketers for bringing in terrible leads, marketers are happy when they bring leads and blame salespeople for not being able to close sales. But what prevents these two realities, in the mature age of digital, from working together as a single entity? If in my business development team, while salespeople "hit the streets," I could bring warm and well-profiled prospects (as salespeople want them) from digital, perhaps already informed and educated, trying to close them automatically and passing only those I can't close to salespeople, thus saving them a lot of time and effort and providing them all the ingredients ready to be served, and then with a mix of automation/adv retargeting/automatic or human CRM, I boosted sales and business metrics, again using salespeople only in critical cases? Would marketing and sales still be separate channels? Do I still sound crazy?

There can no longer be a world where sellers don't want to talk to "marketers," each going their own way, each with different objectives, each massaging their own numbers with different evaluation criteria, without ever sharing what should be the primary value of both jobs: the development of the business of the enterprise.

I am firmly convinced that it's time to stop thinking of it as a competition between marketing and sales and start thinking in terms of Digital Business Development: a context in which, aided by digital, marketing and sales work as a single entity, with the same timing and cycles, constantly sharing macro and micro objectives, the same budget, and the same responsibilities, supporting each other to achieve short, medium, and long-term goals.

1.6 B2B APPROACH VS. B2C APPROACH

Not only startups but also SMEs and especially corporates often define their customers as either B2B or B2C. From this, and from the disambiguation of the concept of "marketing" discussed above, stems the biggest misalignment on the content of the term "marketing" in current times.

A few months ago, I was having gin and tonics with the innovation team of Deloitte Italy. They were launching a startup acceleration program in a "protected environment," and I had engaged them to explore possibilities for collaboration. Very smart people, and unusually competent (I normally distrust consulting firms). After the quick, customary introductions, they hit their first snag: by the very nature of the acceleration program - where the protected environment is formed by financial investors and corporates interested in investing to bring innovation internally - the startups they are selecting are all B2B. For me, there is no friction, I am used to working over 75% in B2B, but in their view, there is no particular marketing to do in B2B. As already mentioned, these are very smart and competent people. So why this perception gap of the same object (marketing)? Simply because no one has ever pointed out to them that the word "marketing" can no longer refer to today's digital approach, that it can no longer be set in opposition to the word "sales". The general belief is that digital marketing is a set of tools and software to be used with an approach (in the best case) more or less scientific. This is why it is identified with B2C: masses of people to be reached with a single message, with many channels and different costs to reach them, because in Italy we are 60 million and in the world 7.5 billion, and it is impossible to speak with everyone one-on-one. This is the greatest legacy of traditional marketing: number of points per number of exposures (what we today call "impressions").

In an "above the line" campaign, I produce coordinated material, declined in several tools and coherent within itself, invest my entire budget in production and media buying, an expense that is planned based on presumed audience on sample statistical data and the number of exposures obtained per person (some still use the magic number of seven - "after seven exposures, the customer buys"). In an attempt to reach my presumed target within a larger cluster - e.g., high school students - with hundreds of thousands of users, of which I evaluate no measurable return. In this perspective, digital marketing seems exclusively an executive tool for campaign distribution: instead of TV, radio, and billboards, use Facebook and YouTube to interact, instead of with "high school students", with my precise target which is "16-year-old high school girls", moreover spending enormously less. And maybe I put a couple of "growth hackers" in so that it takes on a more scientific semblance and we can talk about numbers and do more experiments. All, perhaps, handed over to an agency - which obviously does not share the business objectives of the client but has its precise objective of billing the client as much as possible for the least possible hassle, but that's another story.

Still, in this perspective, digital marketing can make sense for a B2C business, while it is not initially clear how to use it in a B2B business.

The point is that "digital marketing", today, does not mean (or should not mean) this. I propose another perspective: my target is retail points of a specific sector, for example: florists. Fifteen thousand in Italy. My business is entirely B2B, I sell goods to retail points, and it also has the average order value of a B2B business (not the 20€ average receipt of the florist, but 1.5k€ average monthly order of a store). Following the approach of "there are less than a million people, I don't need marketing to interact with them", do you have any idea how long it takes to contact fifteen thousand retail points one by one? Do you have any idea how much humans cost between pre-sales, sales, and account management even just on fifteen thousand measly retail points in Italy?

It turns out that florists, besides being legal entities, are managed by people. In most cases, by one person per point of sale. And exactly like a person, the owner can be inserted into the distribution loop (I contact you and propose stuff automatically until you bite), passing through the entry into the conversion funnel (the series of steps that lead you to become a customer), up to the maintenance loop (automations of management, retention, and cross/up-selling). Removing the 30-50% of humans normally involved in the process, greatly tightening the timelines, dedicating resources only to the most immediate closures, lowering costs, leaving ample margin for corrections along the way, and leaving in history a ton of data that would otherwise be lost like dust in the wind.

Don't like florists? Prefer Project Managers of medium businesses and corporates? In this case, is the customer the corporates or the people working inside them who make decisions? Or maybe the customer is the one who physically has to go to the decision-maker and propose the product? Even in this case, the customer is not "a company," it's a person. And like all people, they can be categorized in a more or less precise cluster, or even identified individually, and inserted into a loop.

Digital marketing is not "marketing with metrics." It's digital support for business development. And business development does not follow different market rules just because "it's B2B": between sending a salesperson on the road from ten leads in a month and sending them to push closures from ten informed and educated prospects, the difference is world-changing. Especially when, perhaps, more than 30% of the closure is done without the use of a salesperson.

In the section on mindset and methodology, I will try to explain with practical case examples how to move away from the "B2B vs B2C" perspective and start thinking of your customers first and foremost as people.

2. MINDSET

2.1 BACKGROUND

Since I'm not an enlightened guru, Ignition is based on some principles of methodologies and frameworks already created by very intelligent people before me, particularly The Lean Startup, Scrum, and, more mildly, Google's OKRs. Since there is a huge amount of literature on these topics, I will not use this opportunity to delve into them, but I will give a quick brief and recommend some preliminary readings. Although the concepts I will describe in the third section are applicable and extendable to one's case even without prior experience, I still believe it is very useful to have at least a basic understanding of the more articulated methodologies that form the foundation of this framework.

"The Lean Startup" by Eric Ries (available almost

everywhere, including Amazon, in the original language or various translations) is a methodology designed for the rapid development and management of startups, not understood as entities but as a concept: any group of people working towards a common business goal on a project for which there are no historical reference points yet. Therefore, an early-stage startup or a team within a company trying to develop and bring a new product to market. The methodology is based on working in tight and rapid cycles where a prototype is quickly built with the minimum number of features to be tested in the market, the reaction and behavior of a real customer to the product are measured, customer feedback is analyzed and interpreted, and the output is used to "learn", setting new reference points that will form the basis for a second, third, fourth cycle of production, testing, and learning.

The entire methodology is centered on using real feedback, rather than assumptions, and data to make rapid business decisions by iteratively iterating on the product to find a quick market fit without wasting time and resources and, by reducing the error time, increasing the chances of success for a product as long as the context allows spending resources on its development.

In particular, from Lean Startup, Ignition uses the product validation cycles to be sold, e.g., pitch (announcement/landing page/any communication tool), campaign distribution, results evaluation (and interpretation, to be used as a reference point for the second production cycle). Ignition also uses the dualism of "preserve or pivot" (if something works according to the criteria set before an experiment, it is increased and declined, if it does not bring the predetermined results, the object is changed radically) and the concept of "innovation accountability": by tracking metrics and results in the short and medium term and analyzing them, and quickly changing direction or tweaking long-term goals, the risk of failure of a business development strategy can be minimized.

Scrum is a framework for developing, delivering, and maintaining complex products. It is based on taking on a complex development problem (e.g., a large feature of a product), breaking it down into sub-problems, and allocating resources to solve them while continuing to release the highest value product possible with the resources available.

You can imagine it as the antithesis of a "waterfall" process in which an entire project is analyzed and planned beforehand, deadlines are given for different milestones based on the problems hypothesized in the preliminary analysis phase, and the development team members remain routinely stuck waiting for the solution from other team members to unanticipated problems, thus bursting every single timeline predicted in the project - sound familiar?

In Scrum, each feature and related problems in realizing it are taken individually, and features are put into production in short cycles, while the team is focused as an entity and not as a single execution on the completion of the work designed within the cycle.

The result is a product in constant release and always

usable by the end user, its continuous improvement during development, and constant control/possibility of modification of team and work environment, processes, objectives, and priorities.

Although Scrum was originally thought in the early '90s mainly for developing, releasing, maintaining, and improving software products, the processes and techniques of the framework can be used and adapted to almost any type of work that includes design, development, and execution. In my career, I have seen Scrum used in the context for which it was designed, but I have also seen it adapted to more "business" contexts such as the application of the framework in the acceleration phase of startups, its use as a management tool for non-software projects, or as a control and delivery tool for routine but cyclically defined jobs such as, even, the management of an entire accounting firm of about twenty people.

From Scrum, Ignition uses the cycle management techniques ("sprints"), the concept of using a team as a single entity that concentrates efforts on the goal rather than as single human resources, the instance of individual problems in a "masterplan" and the concentration of resources in solving sub-problems within a cycle, management based on continuous improvements and adjustments to the medium and long-term plan derived from empirical experience gained within each production cycle.

To learn more about Scrum, you can download its human knowledge (and possibly test your knowledge) on www.scrumguides.org and www.scrum.org.

OKRs (Objectives and Key Results) are a method used by Google to define extremely ambitious objectives (to the point that by definition they must seem unattainable), "explode" them into more sub-objectives (key results that, strung together, lead to achieving the objective) to plan the execution of a plan, and keep track of the journey towards the final goal.

The OKR system, conceived by Andrew Grove, former CEO of Intel, is a shared objectives system based on two fundamental questions that form the basis of its setup:

a) Where do I want to go? The answer to this question provides the final objective;

b) How do I calibrate myself to understand if I am getting there? The answer to this question provides the hypothetical milestones, or rather the "key results";

In the early 2000s, one of Google's first investors began testing OKRs for a couple of quarters within the team. To this day, Google uses annual and quarterly OKRs, and holds extended team meetings each quarter to share and evaluate OKRs.

Boiling it down to the essence, the philosophy behind OKRs is that non-ambitious macro-goals are not valid goals, to the extent that, as a criterion for evaluating progress, it is not expected that the team will achieve more than 60-70% of short-term goals, while achieving more than 70% of the goals means either extraordinary performance or that the goal was too unambitious. Often in my career, I have clashed against two major fronts: the phalanx of senseless and unachievable goals that, however, demanded their achievement and lashed out at the team in case of failure (observing a global failure of the project), and those who set realistic and all too achievable short-term goals. I discovered OKRs only recently, to my surprise finding that I had already, as a result of a ton of experiences, come to share their philosophy. Especially with startups and especially in the initial phase of acceleration, for example, I have learned that goals are almost never achieved: something, especially in conditions of uncertainty, always goes wrong. Always. So if it's true that an ambitious (albeit realistic) goal will never be achieved, it's also true that the effort to achieve it always produces results that would hardly have been achieved with a more "soft" goal.

A couple of very small and superficial but always valid examples:

a) A startup selling a SaaS (Software as a Service) has the goal, starting from zero and to make some sense to a potential investor, of reaching its first thousand users in three months. In the first two-week cycle, the goal is set to make ten. In the second sprint, to make another ten. In the third, to make twenty in a single sprint. By the sixth week, it has hit all its goals, has actually good growth and is convinced it's doing great, but it's not counting on the final goal which, at this rate, it will never reach. By starting to raise the level of goals (e.g., a hundred users in the fourth sprint, more than the total of users acquired in three cycles), after initial discouragement, the team gets creative to start finding further viable paths towards the key-result even with scarce economic and temporal resources available. It doesn't reach the result, but it manages to acquire in just two weeks the number of users it took a month and a half to acquire. And, in trying to reach the result, it creates enough entropy to generate a ton of new learnings and ideas to improve the product in the following cycles, as well as new awareness and knowledge of its market that allows revising the medium-term planning and execution of new strategies;

b) A B2B SME has calculated that, maintaining a rhythm of acquiring about ten new clients each month, and maintaining the Churn Rate (the rate of customer abandonment in the medium/long term) as per its history, it will be able to achieve almost a 20% growth in turnover over the course of a year. An apparently ambitious goal. If it weren't for the fact that the goal was confused with the "key results". Result: by the ninth month, the team is hitting the goal every quarter and is pumped up, but the company is maintaining exactly the same turnover as the previous year due to unforeseen causes (key accounts collapsing, a higher Churn Rate than expected, the physiological reduction of the ARPU (Average Revenue Per User) given the new economic conditions of the market it operates in. By confusing the goal with the key results to be achieved, the team dedicated itself to executing the "little task" evaluating it as a series of successes, but losing sight of the "big picture" (the 20% increase in turnover in a year). Having had that as a clear and shared macro-goal, and evaluating the distance from the point of arrival along the way, the team could have activated to seek further paths (at any level: business, marketing, product) and set other medium-term goals or other key results that would have led them maybe not to hit such an ambitious goal, but at least a still substantial increase in turnover despite the new conditions that had arisen along the way.

From OKRs, Ignition uses long-term planning broken down in the medium term, the definition of key results in the short term and, relying on principles of Scrum, the execution to achieve them, as well as the moment of evaluating the "track-record" as an opportunity to set new OKRs (whether long or medium term).

To delve deeper into the topic, you can go to https://rework.withgoogle.com/guides/set-goals-with-okrs/steps/introduction/ while to practically test the setup of OKRs you can visit http://okrexamples.co/).

2.2 YOU DON'T REALLY KNOW YOUR CUSTOMER

Heavy words, I know. Let's put it this way: when you know your customer perfectly and what they need, you are in a scaling phase: you already have all the ingredients and metrics you need, you know the levers to use, you know how to acquire early adopters and the different (if there are different ones) funnels to convert interested but colder users into customers, and maybe even initially uninterested users. With all this material in hand, you can afford to set optimization goals (e.g., reducing CAC, or increasing the number of sales or the LtV of customers) and work only on those. The common case, however, is that every year there are new products to sell on which you don't have all the reference points available, that the market changes, that within the same product there are new features to sell, that even the type of customer for the same product changes. And, regardless of the phase, from early-stage startups to corporates, it is not uncommon nearly thirty years since the 1990s, for the conditions of uncertainty just mentioned to occur in groups and even several times during the year. And when there is a condition of uncertainty, one must go down like Socrates: know that you do not know. For two major reasons.

The first is negative: where can the arrogance of believing you have understood an object (the customer) that by definition hides a number of parameters in continuous variation - especially depending on the goal - and, above all, in continuous evolution in the market, lead you? A market made up of more or less heterogeneous people in constant personal change who buy other products also in constant variation.

I stopped counting years ago the number of times I heard the phrase "my customer is this, thinks this, wants that." I heard it said about consumers of food supplements, company managers, consumers of old but rich and bored design, on bars/snack bars, on events, on users of audio/video productions, up to, to mention a couple of stranger ones, restaurants in Germany and food importers in Japan, and on other clusters, I believe now well over a few hundred considering that every client or potential one has, at the very least, a couple. My question, since I was less than twenty-five years old, has always been: "if you already know everything, how did we end up at this table, you and I?" Most of the time, especially when I was starting out, the answer could be translated into the fact that we were there because an execution of the "masterplan" was necessary, which the person I was facing was not able to carry out autonomously. Not too different from the work, let's say, of a carpenter: this is the vision, these are the requirements, this is the project, someone is needed to realize it, perhaps adding their own touch. Which then is the main approach of companies to agencies, and the reason why every company, in its entire life, screws up with agencies. Agencies do not share the business objectives of their clients because they already have their own business objective: win the tender, perform the work with the least possible number of problems, possibly getting paid regularly for the invoices and managing to make some kind of upsell to the client.

When I started getting my hands dirty on SME or corporate clients, I had no experience that would allow me to question how the world turned especially in an era when things, simply, "were done that way and that's it" and "the customer wanted it for yesterday", so I always immersed my hands in guano and tried to execute the masterplans I found in front of me, which more than "rough plans" seemed to be scripts of a bad play.

It always turned out that the gigantic plan to stick to was full of gaps and assumptions passed off as solid realities by the person who had produced them, generally a figure who in life aspired to the position of "oracle" or who had inherited the truth from one or more oracles higher up in the organization chart. The plan showed signs of failure from the start, but was carried forward with minimal variations only to flip the responsibility onto the last link in the chain: the plan worked, it was the people involved who were not able to execute it as hypothesized.

I have never seen this attitude vanish: even in companies with a truly innovative product and structure like a startup with investments behind it, there always came a time when I heard the words "it has to be done this way because it converts more." More compared to what? And why? How long will it take to set it up? How much time will we dedicate to applying it before realizing if it works or not? What criteria will we use to tell ourselves whether it is working or not? All generally unanswered questions.

Because the worst thing that can happen when starting from the assumption of knowing every variable perfectly, or at least the most important ones, is to produce universally tangible results but not reach the goals or, worse, not having goals to reach. Starting from the assumption of "having understood," especially without short-term goals but even with them, just producing sales will mean an "I was right" (never an "I was wrong" because numbers, without references, are interpretable) and a tenacity on the plan in an attempt to improve its conditions. An example? Defined a customer a priori (e.g., a restaurant point of sale), if proposing to the potential customer the technological aspect of the product, instead of the agile aspect of the service generated by the product, generates sales, whoever came up with the idea will tend to emphasize it, confirming that they are on the right track, and then will ask those who have to execute the vision to arrive with the technique at goals that, perhaps, are physiologically unreachable. Distinctly putting both UVPs (Unique Value Propositions) on the track, instead, and having set some metrics to monitor and results to achieve (e.g., "number of sales in a quarter" or "reduction of customer acquisition cost"), allows in the short term to choose a path to follow that seems simpler to walk in function of the result.

If the goal is an LtV of 11k€ per year and with one UVP I am fishing for people who seem to be worth less than half, I will probably have to change the type of customer (and, perhaps, also the UVP). If by changing UVP and customer I see the LtV of 11k€ per year as achievable, I cannot expect to produce the volume of sales that I could have produced on customers worth less than half, nor to maintain the same acquisition cost. Nor can I evaluate the performance of a UVP without choosing goals in priority (also chronological priority, if desired). We are taught as children that you can't have your cake and eat it too. As adults, that you can't judge a fish by its ability to climb a tree. So why should I negatively evaluate the CAC if I am exceeding the sales volume goal, while the same CAC or slightly less would be fine with lower volumes but a higher LtV, achievable perhaps with another UVP?

The second reason why the application of the philosophy of "you don't know your customer" is not a triviality to be taken for granted, is the opportunity: starting from constant exploration allows moving freely in an environment made up of long-term goals, with the possibility of verifying their validity (and eventually modifying them) in the medium term, using short-term goals as validation references.

As long as the plan is made fluid and there is the ability to modify business goals along the way, the assumption of trying different paths with equal evaluation criteria (the goals to be achieved) allows creating a history of data to be used for new hypotheses and having a wider range of options to reach the really important goals, discarding or shelving, perhaps, the less urgent ones.

A startup at any stage, for example, by definition operates in a freer environment: the main goal is to attract investments in the next round, so profit becomes just a reflection of the business goals required to close that round. An example: when a startup begins to structure itself and the work is no longer carried out only by the founders, the business goals begin to evaporate as they are transmitted from person to person along the execution chain. Ask the "digital marketing specialist" - an employee who physically manages the digital adv campaigns - of a startup with even a few million behind it if, by chance, he has an idea of why he is doing what he does, and what the company's objectives are. On average, you will find yourself in front of a person who at best tries to respect the KPIs that have been parameterized for him, thinking he is doing his job poorly when the acquisition of a customer is costing him more than the value of the customer's first order, totally ignoring that not only is the goal for investors to reach a certain number of customers to show market penetration, but also to reach an LtV not even exaggeratedly high and, in that precise phase, even potentially going into break-even. The same person will not understand, if business goals are not shared with him, why only three months later he is asked to quickly find a way to take the same volume of turnover with an extremely lower CAC, without even being able to explain why it is impossible or being able to give his solution to the fact that the goal of "moving to a higher LtV" can be achieved in another way (for example using a particular channel with a different UVP).

Sharing business goals with the team and, in the reverse channel, sharing the work of the teams evaluating them on business goals, allows rowing the boat in the same direction and with the same intensity, keeping the field free for variations of medium-term goals that lead to achieving long-term goals.

Not having reference points means working to create them while trying to achieve business goals. Creating them quickly and easily means exponentially increasing one's knowledge by creating data and small stories of success or failure. Having those stories and clashing them with medium-term goals allows analyzing the trend with respect to long-term goals and changing strategies several times along the way to reach them.

Taking more paths instead of one or two, quite simply, allows for more chances of success: betting on a single number does not have the same odds of winning as betting on twenty numbers. The intellect of the team should serve, more than to handle Google and Facebook Ads, to understand how to use the budget in hand to simultaneously try more bets and what it takes, at a minimum, to put those bets on the table in the shortest possible time.

2.3 SAME TEAM, SAME GOALS

One of the most disarming legacies that, in my opinion, we carry from before the maturity of digital is the separation into almost stagnant compartments of the marketing and sales teams, in an eternal race of who has more muscle but in a context where the only competition should be against the market and competitors, finding more efficient and rapid ways to use the available budget to achieve the best results. Digital is not a skill: it is a tool that should be used to facilitate the use of people's skills by reducing times and distances and allowing the rapid construction of a context in which it becomes easier to operate, so as to have more time available to achieve goals with the same human resources employed.

We are talking about "business development." Do marketing and sales really follow different objectives in the macro-goal of business development? Does the sales team really have to be evaluated exclusively in terms of the number of deals closed regardless of the sales cycle, and does the marketing team really have to be evaluated in the number of leads generated and their cost or, in the most tragic of contexts, in ephemeral KPIs of "awareness"? Do sales really develop business in the short/medium term while marketing works in the long term? And what if, instead, the members of the two teams worked together with shared objectives? If "a hundred new clients with an average LtV of 10k€ per year" is the company's goal, why can't marketing and sales work together trying to help each other and changing their modulation along the race to the common goal? I have never had the real opportunity to bring this mentality to a corporate, while I have managed to square its application in seed-stage startups (by definition simpler, since those who get their hands dirty with operations are the founders and very few other surrounding resources) and, above all, in SMEs and funded startups that, in the end, have a common context: the founders still have the power to make most of the decisions and the human resources dedicated to business development are still relatively few (and therefore more manageable). Some examples:

a) A funded startup, food sector, B2B clientele (retail points). While the sales team (three fixed people plus others supporting on a spot basis) does over 90% of the dirty work by going on the street and acquiring new clients at a sustained rate of 6-8 clients per month per salesperson and maintaining a 25% closure rate on each potential client, marketing pursues long-term goals still unclear to the company (being a startup) more identifiable with "transmitting corporate values and service strengths" - strengths that are not necessarily recognized as a value for the client, but that the company wants to show.

In the middle, there is an experiment using a commercial human resource to take customer management away from the salespeople and centralize it on a single person (the base of a potential future team) remotely. Simply put: why should every problem or upsell require a visit from a salesperson, who in the sector is also a waste of time for the client, when the same work can potentially be managed by a single contact within the company communicating with the client more with WhatsApp than on the phone?

The business goal of the last quarter of the year is set in terms of generated revenue and sub-KPIs in terms of the volume of new clients acquired for three types: in one, the work of contact by salespeople is almost the only sensible way being few players in the market (work that is worth every penny spent, because each of the clients yields much more than the third type), the second is a hybrid between the first and third in value and type, there are just under ten thousand players in Milan alone but, on the other hand, the engagement methods are not yet clear, the third is a lower level type with several thousand potential clients in a single city, with a lower LtV but for which there is already a more or less defined empirical sales model, the result of the sales team's work that for a year went down to the streets to talk to clients and improved the sales funnel.

While the marketing team struggles even to spend a measly budget of 1k€/month and has no particular data to support whether it is going in the right direction or not (not having objectives), the sales team does an inhuman job and costs as much as fire.

In the perspective of helping the company achieve the business goals of the last quarter, I start from the first concept I consider senseless: the sales team has found its way to acquire new clients, while marketing (even on the company's website) does not follow the sales funnel of the street salespeople, insisting on telling values and features that salespeople do not use because, on the contrary, if they told them they would lose the client by confusing them. I have never quite understood the initial and ongoing resistance in digitizing a sales model that has been found to work on the street (made up of storytelling and defined commercial steps from free trial to regular ordering client), but the result was clear: after three months and some technical setbacks (it's not easy to invent ways and channels to reach that particular client with digital), the marketing team, sometimes with the almost forced assistance of the sales team, influenced the acquisition of new clients by over 30%, contributing to reaching the final goal with just over a month to spare. Although a lead generated by marketing is (then confirmed by closure rates) more informed and educated ("hot", in technical terms) and therefore more quickly closable by the sales team compared to the work of "one-to-one" engagement from entering the retail point to the recurrence of orders, it would still be wrong to see the task of marketing as mere procurement of hot leads to support sales. What prevents, for example, closing clients automatically by improving the communication flow (thus not stopping at leads but going further with automatic communication to the client), using the "man in the middle" (the account dedicated to post-sales management) also for closing new clients if necessary, and using human intervention and the skills of a physical salesperson in case of urgency and/or high value of the potential client?

In a scheme that I only managed to define but was then set aside for a major shift in focus to very high-profile clients, based on facts and data actually recovered during that quarter, abandoning the logic of "marketing vs sales", the work of the "business development team" should have followed this flow:

1. Salespeople dedicate themselves to a higher level of clientele (the hybrid cluster) and, while trying to produce the first stable sales, understand what the client perceives as value and what are the steps that make the sales funnel more fluid on that cluster;

2. Marketing takes over the lower value cluster entirely, working on volumes (despite the B2B nature of the product) and trying to automate the acquisition funnel, using part of the time of the human resource dedicated to CRM only if necessary (client not closed in "self-service");

3. Marketing sends a physical salesperson in case the estimated value of the client is very high or in case of a problem (e.g., client who has stopped ordering);

4. Marketing begins to experiment with UVPs also on the hybrid cluster to which salespeople are dedicating themselves, providing them with leads to validate in the field (it is not certain that they provide valid leads);

5. Salespeople, aware that they do not have to necessarily use the UVPs proposed by marketing and, indeed, have to vary them in an attempt to understand something, regularly return to the fold with new feedback on their attempted acquisitions, what seems to work and what does not, and on the quality of the leads brought by digital. This does not mean passing by the office occasionally between one client and another saying "one today told me that you have to change the image on the site". It means giving yourself method, context, and time to coordinate everyone's activities, share the feedback received, and plan the following actions;

6. Once the model validated "on the street" by the salespeople is defined, begin to automate everything to free up a lot of their time and allow increasing the pace with the same resources and budget employed;

All this using a spending model based on a budget shared with everyone, in which the acquisition of a client can be calculated in relation to both the expenses of campaign distribution and the time used by salespeople for each single client, relating it to the LtV and understanding what to automate and how to provide mutual support in the perspective of achieving the annual business goals (long term), reorganizing in the medium term (semester) and planning actions in the short term (quarters).

b) Seed-stage startup, import and distribution of flowers and accessories from the Netherlands to retail points (florists). The case in which I have had the most opportunity to mix marketing and sales into a single model where you no longer ask yourself "is this the role of marketing or sales?" and in which both skills have mixed in the team supporting each other.

The big opportunity in this case, as far as I am concerned, was being part of it from the first hour. I had already followed the startup in the previous months when it was trying to build a flower delivery service (like Interflora) that made economic sense, and in the attempt to acquire its own network of florists I had clashed along with the founders with a very aged sector and logics rooted in the greatest of common legacies: "it has always been done this way". Having to deal with florists and with their product, we came across their "pain" with the product, with those who supplied it to them and even, by pure chance, with the players who acted as importers and wholesalers in Italy.

The flower delivery model, after a few months, seemed to take some kind of sense but not with the rhythms and KPIs that were being demanded by potential investors, so I pushed the team a lot to "pivot" the shack on B2B: why couldn't we use the same digital techniques on florists instead of the end consumer, margining much more with the same customer, albeit at the price of changing much of the work to be done?

The traditional chain of this sector, still today,

includes:

1. Purchase by exporters of the product at auction in the Netherlands;

2. Collection, storage in the warehouse, and export of the product to wholesalers in Europe (in our case in Italy);

3. Collection and storage in the warehouse by local Italian wholesalers;

4. Sale and distribution to florists in the territory (in attempted direct sale to the store, or by phone, or physically in "cash and carry" mode);

We started with the new model at the end of August with the only Dutch exporter who had not immediately slammed the door in our face, branding us as losers, discovering that our supplier (a large Dutch exporter) was exactly trying to eat up the role of the importer and that of the local wholesaler, selling directly to florists through a digital platform that, in reality, had a structure not at all suitable for florists as it had been designed to facilitate the order to importers and wholesalers.

Anyone in the sector, since the flower delivery experiment, had told us that the human relationship with the retail point is fundamental in this business, and therefore without a sales network we would not go anywhere. In the meantime, however, without going into detail about the techniques used, we had already been able to acquire at a sustained rate florists who wanted to enter our flower delivery network, without ever having to leave the office with a suitcase like a traveling salesman.

We thought it could be an excellent initial funnel: engage the retail point with the excuse of flower delivery, serve the retail point with incoming orders or with peer-to-peer orders from the same acquired florists, and then step in with a "dear customer, since you trust us because we brought you money, what if we told you that we also sell wholesale flowers?".

It worked. Simply because we had no other means, we had no particular goals yet other than to start selling, and because by definition a contact already served listens to you more than a contact yet to be created. The effort was immense: two of the founders, for an entire month, spent their days on the phone moving deals and contacts on Hubspot trying to close the first orders. There was already a sort of automation of the process: florists, from campaigns on multiple channels, registered autonomously leaving a lot of information useful to us to understand the economic value of the retail point and focus on those of higher value (a flower shop can order from 300€ to over 5k€ of goods per month) and were automatically synchronized in Hubspot, ready to be worked on by an operator. But the pace was very low and the commercial effort exaggerated. We started working on automations: why spend time on the phone instead of working automatically on the hottest leads using email and messages on WhatsApp Business? The engagement operations dropped significantly to the point of being able to dedicate a single resource to the closures of the first sales, receiving the hottest profiles, also helped by the fact of cutting completely the part of the funnel of the flower delivery and going directly to the sale of goods from the Netherlands: we received many fewer leads, but they were leads much hotter.

Over time and with the increase in operations to manage the few clients as they entered, we decided to "roughly" automate some additional commercial steps by having the user profile himself, gradually discovering the information he needs and opening an account autonomously, focusing the commercial effort only on the last barrier to entry.

To date, having closed the first phase of business development and arrived in the seed-stage, the acquisition of florists still works with a patchwork with automated flows between Typeform, a chatbot, both synchronized with Hubspot which, depending on the status of the client or potential client, communicates automatically reminders via WhatsApp and manages most of the acquisition and maintenance via chatbot, maintaining the use of an operator via chat or phone only if necessary.

In this really non-technical process, the two sides of the blanket that continuously uncovered each other in an attempt to find a balance, were the quality of the service and the price of the goods. The only way to initially keep the quality low while waiting to build on a digital product that would make it excellent compared to market standards was to keep a price so low as to allow easy acquisition at the expense of a service with all its gaps and limitations. Keeping a low price, however, meant having less economic resources available and potentially remaining excessively stuck on business development at a later time. The mix of "human" engagement with the client, various attempts at price, audience, and UVP, allowed us in a short time to triple (and maintain in growth) the pace of acquisition while maintaining a price that allowed us to apply a 20% margin on the goods (against the 30-40% of competitors) creating space to generate additional future margin once the import, stock, and logistics processes were made efficient and digitized (seed-stage of the project).

Not only that: dealing with clients and automating some of the internal processes, allowed us to identify a ton of additional client pains and to design automated digital solutions that could serve as subsequent UVPs useful for acquiring more clients at a higher rate and bringing each client to a higher expense each month.

At the time of writing, the startup is, indeed, in the seed-stage. While I hope to be able to write about its developments in a future edition of Ignition, what I can say is that the method, the technique, and the initial speed (both of acquisitions and of the development of each single order per client, both the entity of the orders) were the three "off-market" parameters that pushed our first supplier (unlike the others, also competitors) to take an interest in the project and understand how to apply the same "machine" to his attempt at direct sales and distribution from the Netherlands to the florist. In a world where there are still commercial agents who use so much of their time and effort to destroy the company's margins on the product, a forced execution (due to a lack of human and financial resources) of mixed marketing and sales has led to the definition of a model in which people are added to the team based on the skills needed at the moment and only based on the actual increase in volume of clients to be managed and not, vice versa, "a priori" to be able to acquire clients - then, anyway, to be managed - automating everything that is possible with the resources at hand at that moment and working as a single block of "commercial operations" in function of the company's macro-objectives.

How much was it due to marketing? How much to sales? No one asked themselves, because the main purpose of sales was exactly to automate their processes both in providing their own leads and in their management. Because, who said that a salesperson cannot also use digital marketing to sell better (and more)?

In the section on the "rules" and techniques of Ignition, I will try to rationalize how the members of the business development team can interact with each other using the same timing, the same metrics, and the same objectives.

2.4 ENOUGH WITH "B2B vs B2C"

In the section on the problems of digital business

development which Ignition tries to address, I delved into the legacy of "our business is B2B, we don't need marketing". Although I have already had the chance to describe some examples where marketing played a fundamental role despite dealing with B2B products, it's probably useful to have a clear understanding of some cases to better comprehend the approach. The fundamental concept to understand at the threshold of the end of the first two decades of the 2000s is that digital is a tool and the internet is used by people. And if it's true that companies are made of people, those same people use the internet and, therefore, can be reached with the same exact techniques used for promoting B2C products. Alternatively, at the most rudimentary level, digital can be used to streamline and facilitate the work of teams tasked with "finding" and engaging those people.

An example: a seed-stage startup that sells virtual sales networks to its clients (companies). I won't delve into the B2B client acquisition in this case, but rather focus on the acquisition of salespeople to offer on the platform. Try this mental exercise: how and where can I find commercial agents or similar figures willing to sell third-party products? The profile type is perfectly comparable to B2B: commercial agents are everywhere and are completely different individuals. Some have a technological background, others in fashion; some are graduates, others are not; some were salespeople for a company, others have never done anything similar before; some are registered in some roster, others are "business finders" not found on any list; there are fat and thin ones, fans of one team or another, living in very different locations, with different turnovers, some with families and others without, and so on indefinitely. Yet they are people: they can receive my communications, it's all about identifying them as efficiently as possible to be able to acquire them with the available budget, and communicating the right UVP to bring them on board.

Until my arrival, the startup recruited sellers by insisting with DEM (Direct Email Marketing) through a site that claimed to have over thirty thousand users all profiled as commercial agents. As I started dealing with the sector, some ideas emerged that, through attempts and failures, became the new acquisition model. I won't delve into the UVPs or the steps of the funnel, I'll limit myself to the use of channels:

1. LinkedIn. I know what you're thinking (because it's the first thing everyone thinks): advertising on LinkedIn with an audience based on job titles. No. I still haven't quite understood why, but despite the immense potential of LinkedIn, the advertising aspect of the platform is still very rudimentary and generates, up to the time of writing, results that could be euphemistically described as "disarming". Moreover, LinkedIn's tools for recruiting in that sector yielded low volumes at very high costs (I still haven't understood why sellers didn't react well to job offers).

Trying to scrape emails by combining the use of some

tools and LinkedIn's Sales Navigator, however, I realized that as the scraper opened the profiles of my "victims" it generated a visit notification that these profiles received under "here's who viewed your profile". On one hand, I found relatively few emails to insert into a presentation funnel for the platform (about 15-20% of the total available contacts were valid and usable), on the other hand, within a week my profile had received dozens of connection requests from these sellers, probably driven by the anxiety of finding clients seeing that I was working for a platform that - coincidentally - offered them products to sell.

The evolution of the technique was relatively simple: create a profile specifically for recruiting maximizing the space offered by LinkedIn with useful information for the sellers to be recruited, combining scraping with organic requests generated during the process, to whom I would copy-paste further information for registration just like in the email funnel. In essence, use a personal page as if it were a landing page for lead generation.

2. Google Ads. If it's true that sellers are looking for products to sell, there would probably be search phrases useful for identifying them and offering them registration on a platform where they can find those products. The work on this channel followed a more "technical" and "by the book" process of identification and optimization, eventually producing a low volume of registered users but with a decent acquisition cost, contributing at least 30% to the total volume of

acquired users. The moral here is not to get stuck on a single channel where performance reaches a physiological "cap", but to consider it as a piece of the model that, at a low cost, contributes to leveling the general acquisition costs while contributing a decent percentage to the overall acquisition.

3. Facebook. Who said that to find sellers (and potential ones) useful for reselling third-party products in a "multi-mandate" mode, you only need specifically targeted multi-mandate commercial agents or that, to find such niche profiles at a decent cost, they must be targeted with such deep detail? Various mixed clusters of age, interests, and some work variables can give access to a world that not only includes commercial agents but also those who still don't know they could do that job despite having the skills. For example, at the end of the first quarter, Facebook contributed about 40% of global acquisitions, almost all of which were profiles not currently active as commercial agents: they were the product of people of the right age to get involved, with a background and interest in sales of any kind, from insurance agents to "wannabe" network marketers. The fact that these profiles were also the most responsive to the sale of third-party products, added a gem to the entire business model of the startup, which in the following months closed with sales mandates and

began to sell offline lead generation.

2.5 DIY (DO IT YOURSELF) AND AUTOMATIONS

If you know your product, the right UVP (Unique Value Proposition) for a specific customer cluster, your customer's potential objections (and have learned to manage them), you are able to sell your product. Probably, at that point, you can also sell it using digital means. If, on the other hand, you don't know precisely how to sell your product, digital won't be of any help. Digital is not the end, it's the means: using digital tools to automate or scale workflows can help scale the business by optimizing time and costs (and keeping human resources employed in the processes to a minimum). Digital is a support to work, so you still need to know how to do your job. A quite classic example:

a) A B2B SME in the food sector, which has already approached digital. Poor performance marketing, unexciting sales performance except for a single salesman. The guideline for the year is to squeeze marketing performance (digital) to compensate for the costs and volumes of sales without having to hire more salespeople. Beyond the approach obviously not shared by me, given what I've written so far, in this case, the fundamental error is imagining digital as the solution. Does it work poorly? "Squeeze it more" to make it work, so I can continue to spend on sales without feeling bad. "Make it work". Out of nowhere. Just like that. Senselessly.

It turns out that the only salesman with decent performance is also the only one not using the "sales script" imposed by the company on the other salespeople. He uses different UVPs for different types of customers and doesn't convey the values that the company wants to impose to sell those products. And the wonder is that he doesn't even realize the work he has done, in fact, initially, he doesn't talk very willingly about what he has built because, in order to take more bonuses, he has effectively violated some principles dictated by the company.

On the other hand, pointing out the UVPs used by this specific salesman and trying to replicate the same work, the company refuses to use them in marketing (which is nothing but scaling and facilitating the work of salespeople). It demands much better performance while maintaining the same approach. It would be like turning around, firing the salesman with the best performance, and telling the others to sell more but without using the concepts used by the one who, in the end, sold the most. What sense does that make? Yet, to this day, this is one of the most common scenarios, as well as the reason why I no longer work for SMEs and Corporates.

b) A funded startup, again B2B and still in the food sector. On one hand, it echoes the previous example, resisting the use of UVPs used by salespeople and demanding to improve performance while maintaining value propositions that the salespeople don't even talk about. Following a significant increase in performance, one of the founders still complains about the fact that to achieve them (despite the only goal of the period being precisely to achieve those performances) it was proceeded by "mimicking" the sales department instead of going a different way. It's understandable: in his mind, sales and marketing are two separate things, and the fact that they "copy each other", logically, unifies the performances and doesn't allow finding potentially better new ways. The problem is that it's not true.

In fact, the moment comes when a product on a defined customer cluster has its method of sale, good performance, and the sales cycle is sufficiently integrated digitally, thus maintaining costs at the edge of decency, but there is another product (suitable for another customer cluster) that, instead, the salespeople are not able to sell despite continually repeating to each other the value propositions they believe to be solid and the fact that customers are idiots and don't understand them. In this case, replicating the work and knowledge of sales on digital would be by definition a suicide, even though out there there is still someone convinced of the fact that "if it doesn't work on the street, maybe it does online", while on the marketing side it's possible to test many different UVPs on many recipients spending two cents and putting relatively little time. In two or three days, you can interpret the results of a small test campaign (whose goal is, therefore, not to sell but to understand which concepts pull more), put the new ideas in the hands of the salespeople and start testing in the field (in a more qualitative way) the effectiveness of the new arguments to focus on, or give input on how to choose the clients to "attack". After a constant increment (obtained with teamwork between sales and marketing) of the sales model, the flow could go back and marketing could scale the model validated by sales while continuing to test new different value propositions. In this case, who copied from whom? In a similar case, would marketing and sales have worked together by putting their skills at the disposal of the goal?

A significant part of the potential of digital is given by the possibility of automating human work. A substantial part of the work of digital business development (I could estimate it at 25%) should focus on automations. You start a new workflow, test it, find your first customer. What's the point of restarting or using the same cycle a million times with the same resources employed? Automating as much as possible within the workflow can allow you, for example, to manage ten thousand leads at a time instead of ten. All without even needing particular IT knowledge or skills: out there is full of pre-packaged tools that can help automate your work.

An example of heavy and progressive automation: an early-stage startup, B2B in the floriculture sector (flowers), team composed only of the two founders. The first intuition is that by calling florists and offering them a free service they can profile them, activate them and start gaining trust to then, in a second part of the funnel, become their suppliers of flowers, plants, and accessories. The intuition is not wrong, but managing the calls is very "time-consuming" and the initially planned funnel is quite long, so no immediate indicators on the result are seen. They decide, therefore, to use digital: beyond the techniques used on which I will not elaborate here, they profile and bring florists from Facebook to a TypeForm questionnaire to "register" (and thus self-profile). At this point, choosing them based on geography and expected sales volume, one of the founders can concentrate the calls on the hottest and most useful florists at the moment, also decimating the "onboarding" times of the florist.

However, the funnel is still too long and bringing each lead to closure one by one with calls requires several steps. Working eight hours a day only on acquisition, they reach a performance of one new customer per week. They decide to skip a step: the second intuition is that maybe there are florists already ready to buy from us following our value propositions, and there's no real need to go through the proposal of a free service. We use different UVPs and bring the same exact audience to a registration form in which, however, we precisely talk about the supply of flowers, plants, and accessories. The performance obviously drops in volume, but the leads that arrive are by definition the hottest possible, therefore they allow spending less time to bring the lead to closure. With this trick, acquisition goes from one customer a week to three-four a week.

The new problem is that, being the team composed only of the two founders, the one dedicated to acquisition can't dedicate eight hours a day forever to that work. Not having the economic availability to add a human resource for that work, we decide to try to reduce the time spent moving from oral conversation to chat

(WhatsApp and Messenger) and using pre-set and chained messages, and to automate the lead management process (which still requires three or four steps before reaching the end of the funnel and making their first order): we build a ManyChat chatbot that replicates exactly the scheme used "manually" by the founder and sends reminder messages to users who get stuck along the funnel and messages to the operator when a user is close to closure. This way, the "self-service" process of those who are already warmly interested in becoming a customer is sped up without even using a human resource, who intervenes instead only to push down the funnel those who got stuck for some reason that required "human" management of the problem. The chatbot is synchronized with Hubspot, where the various phases of the customer from acquisition to subsequent orders are followed, and Hubspot is synchronized with Messenger and WhatsApp, and sends automatic reminders to customers when they haven't ordered for a while or when they should order but towards the last available hours they still haven't done it. The result is that, without particular technological developments, the volume of customer acquisition remains more or less stable while the physical time dedicated to acquisition is reduced by over 70%, and the heavy management of customers after acquisition is reduced to the point that the operator is involved only when, at sight, he finds anomalies or evident requests for human intervention.

We are talking about an early-stage startup with a team of two people without funds. What prevents anyone else, even a single salesman for himself, from working in the same way?

3. METHODOLOGY

3.1 TRACKING

I often encounter very confused situations regarding the process of "tracking" metrics and results. More often than not, when talking about "tracking data", the responses are "sure, we have Analytics". The point of the matter is not "having a tool that tracks some data", but the concept of tracking data to be able to analyze, use those analyses to interpret the data, and use those interpretations to make decisions on actions to be taken. Tracking data is different from analyzing them, and data analysis is different from interpreting them. Everything that leads to the execution of actions should be guided by analysis and interpretation. And therefore, to the collection of this data. Having a tracking system (Facebook pixel, Analytics tracker, Google Ads performance tracker, whatever you prefer) is different from having a place to store the collected data, only those and no others, in progression and especially in reference to the actions taken. More broadly: having access to some data does not mean you have really tracked those data, especially if they are non-standard data.

If I have key metrics that concern my business, I need to maintain constant calculation of those metrics and need to be able to see their change at a glance over the execution period.

Tracking is not analysis: tracking is the work of calculating and writing down the numbers somewhere in order to preserve them and have a basis for analysis. A couple of examples:

a) A corporate in the fashion industry. I ask for data on sales generated digitally, and I ask both at the national level (Italy and Spain were my two cases of interest) and at the European level (to have a general benchmark that allows me to do the "peasant's accounts"). My contact, two days after the request, gives me as the only data the number of sales (a volumetric data, for me) and the CR (Conversion Rate) from a visitor to the digital store to purchase (number of purchases over number of site visits).

Beyond being terribly brutal (and therefore useless) as a set of metrics, beyond being very vague and insignificant to calculate the global CR (generally, the funnel is broken down into several CRs to understand which phases need work), the data of the global CR is quite strange: they tell me it is 0.1% (they can't tell me if it's at the European or national level and for which of the two countries). Working in my sector, where even when I had the agency I was used to considering any CR below 0.5% as poor performance and vaguely interesting a CR close to 1%, I ask for clarification thinking I had received a wrong figure. It turns out I was right: the data was much worse, their CR was 0.01%.

Apart from the fact that after three years I still haven't had the opportunity to understand if that was the data for a particular country or for the whole of Europe (for the three months I worked there I didn't have direct access to the data), I was very surprised at the lightness with which this data was treated: "yes, sorry, I made a mistake" - and it was one hundredth less. Let's be clear: mathematics and algebra have never had residence in any of my mindsets, but in such a "short" system (from zero to 1% spans the universe), having a performance of x or a value that is a hundred times better or worse than x makes all the difference in the world. This simple confused data, therefore, was treated without any respect, and served only as a number to cite in meetings. 0.05%, depending on the meeting, would probably have made an impression or still seemed terrible, while any of my concerns about "really just you can't stay just below 1%?" would have been laughed off, as an impossible scenario.

The other thing that struck me about this case (precisely because it was very corporate and theoretically very familiar with digital) was the fact that all the rest of the metrics were not shared with any of my contacts. For every more detailed request, someone inside the company had to sift through the data to reconstruct the history and come up with metrics calculated on the fly and, often, with three different results on three different collections of the same data. It didn't strike me that a company like that didn't know how to do that work, because in reality the collection is a simple job that doesn't require particular skills. What hit me hard and straight between the teeth was the fact that a company like that didn't care about very basic metrics for me, and therefore had no way of evaluating the performance of individual actions and the objectives of their long, medium, and let alone short-term plans.

b) An SME in the food sector. I ask for basic digital metrics for what is effectively an e-commerce. I am given some numbers taken "from Analytics" without knowing either when or how, with also a qualitative analysis as a corollary, and at the same time as my request (which I needed to be able to start rationalizing real objectives in the long, medium and short term) I am given an interpretation of the data with consequent objectives to be reached - in short, in the request for information to do my job, I receive the apparent execution of my own job.

The first earthquake shock was the CR and the relative interpretation: declaring a 9% global CR (again, not "from cart to start of checkout", but just "from visitor to purchase"). And the interpretation was "we realize it is very low, this year we would like to raise it to 15%". As a first provocative suggestion, I suggested limiting access to the site to the hot hours of the day. They didn't get the joke and covered me with insults (not even too veiled, I still keep very folkloric e-mails).

The point was not the number, it was the fact that they gave very approximate interpretations at the time of data collection, especially given that - having had direct access to their Analytics later - the data did not represent absolutely anything: in any period and with any initial discrimination, I could not make that 9% come back in my analysis.

At the risk of seeming very slow-minded, I asked for clarification: the answer was that "that 9% was a record of a good day in history" - which I then found out was a single pre-Christmas day two Christmases before, following an offer on a particular commonly used product discounted by 50% compared to the market.

From my "preliminary" analyses (of two minutes), the company had a CR of 3% last year, which - although it was a B2B with very little traffic by definition - surprised me positively. But the moral of the fable is another: doing the tracking, analysis and interpretation work by giving me a piece of data from a particular day far back in time when you decided to sell your goods almost under cost (hiding from me the goal you wanted to achieve at that moment of madness) means giving me a totally distorted view to work on and, above all, it means that you have not done any work, before analysis and interpretation, of collecting that data. In short: you have been "doing things" for two years, but you have not even created the basis to understand what you are doing or why.

3.2 ANALYSIS

You've tracked data and chosen which ones to track, jotting them down in some type of container to mark the progress that interests you. Now, you need to make decisions and plan actions. To do this, there's no escaping it, you need to analyze the data you've collected. Analysis is not simply "looking at the numbers." Analysis means looking at the numbers, asking questions about those numbers, making hypotheses about the answers, and only then using some type of tool (e.g., Google Analytics) to investigate the numbers and find clues that can prove those hypotheses. "Our global CR has dropped in recent days" means nothing. "Why has our global CR dropped while our Average Cart - the average value of individual sales - has almost doubled?" is a starting point for analysis. Could it be due to a change in the campaign's audience or the budget spent? Or perhaps some particular promotion? Or a new product release? For each hypothesis, there is investigative work to be done to verify whether the hypothesis is correct or invalid. This is the work of analysis: the investigation. A couple of examples:

a) An early-stage startup still closing its first seed round (the first round of investments for a startup, a more or less standard phase in the development of a business without historical reference points). I return to work with them after months of them going it alone, and they present me with some apparently striking facts: "At the moment we're averaging about ten sales a month, our CR over the last six months has risen from under 1% to an average of 2%, and that problem with cart additions (below 5% of visitors) we had months ago has been solved, we're now around 15%. Yet we can't push the metrics."

Given these premises, and taking the results of the analyses as valid, even after a counter-analysis, it seemed they had broken through the major barriers encountered months earlier. However, no one on the team could explain or even hypothesize why.

Starting with the first actions from my pure hypotheses (based on the team's sentiments), a week later we maintained the same rates (percentage values) as the previous week: the same CR, the same rate of cart additions, the same number of visitors as the previous week (and month).

Yet, in this first round of just one week, over 75% of those results came from two meager and foolish trial campaigns launched on Facebook just to create new reference points. In other words, they wouldn't have maintained their usual metrics if they hadn't run those two half-baked campaigns. While the question "what value does that data have?" I leave to the section on interpretation, the moral of the story is that the team, in this small case, despite having done a decent job of tracking, didn't ask any questions nor did they investigate: they simply limited themselves to noting the positive change in the data. And the fact that the change was "positive" stopped them from "wasting" time asking why. This prevented them from interpreting the phenomenon. And this prevented them from taking action. Which prevented them from having new reference points. Which led to "floating" in a pond of data generated by the universe, without any further understanding of what was happening. The correct reading of that "pond" should have been: "all this happened and we were not able to understand why and, therefore, to ride the wave taking advantage of the opportunity given to us by the market."

b) An SME in the food sector, directly from the previous paragraph. Those with a 9% CR, to be clear. Their annual goal, hidden from me as I was an outsider because it was a "business goal and therefore internal to the company," that year, was to generate an additional million in revenue.

Producing additional revenue is achievable in dozens of different ways, therefore by definition with a "mix" of actions. To produce more revenue, for example, I can:

- increase the number of customers who order regularly each month;
- increase the average spend per user (at a further level, by increasing the average cart per transaction or seeking monthly upsells for each customer);
- increase the frequency of orders;
- generate more revenue from the logistics service provided to customers;
- dozens of other possible solutions;

It goes without saying that, in this context, if tracking, analysis, and interpretation are badly fused into a single "our CR is 9%, it's low, this year we need to raise it to 15%," it creates a short circuit of useless information that generates divine grace-outside objectives and, moreover, totally useless: to raise the global CR from 9% to 15%, for example, I could limit access to the site only to the "hottest" hours for purchases. In a B2B e-commerce, this would mean providing a disservice to some users but accepting visits from the most motivated users, thus reducing the number of visitors and increasing the number of sales in relation to those visitors. If nine buy on an average day out of a hundred visitors, my CR is 9%. If I reduce those hundred visitors to 60 and keep the nine buyers, my global CR automatically rises to 15%. I haven't changed anything but the CR metric, in fact, I've worsened performance because, for example, I'll be spending the same money at the source to drive traffic (lowering margin and ROI - Return On Investment), maintaining the same average cart (or lower, it might turn out from further analysis that average carts are higher in more "niche" time slots) and, paradoxically, by limiting access at certain times of the day I might generate a medium-term drop in active users (simply because by closing access I create a disservice and therefore a user potentially interested in shopping but who, at the moment, was just looking at the new assortment, won't buy from me in the next month).

"Healing" a metric is not the point: the point is to understand which metrics really need to be taken care of (in function of a goal), and in what proportion so as not to destroy other related metrics. The "how" is up to interpretation but, if analysis is avoided or reduced to an intern exercise, opportunities to act will never be found (see the fact that, in the precise case just narrated: the best customers seemed to be precisely those who ordered by noon, then in the early afternoon there was no correlation between acquired leads and converted customers, while in the early evening the leads generated with the highest conversion rate in the first order made were concentrated). This besides the fact that a 9% global CR would already be excessively positive in itself (and therefore should lead to further questions and other analyses). And this besides the fact that, anyway, as seen in the previous paragraph, that "9% to be raised to 15%" was not even a real data: nevertheless, the entire company boasted of moving "at the pace of metrics" using one calculated "ad hoc" by someone in the company who simply wanted to look good.

3.3 INTERPRETATION

Data is indicative, not objective: To observe data, all you need is to look at it, but to read it, interpretation is necessary. Merely looking at numbers, even finding correlations among them, is not enough to take action. Probably, our best shot at "getting it right" lies in the approach: building, not alone but with your team, hypotheses based on intuition and investigating these by finding numbers that can corroborate them. Having at your disposal a set of multiple hypotheses validated (or invalidated) by the data can lead you to see a "bigger picture" of the puzzle on which to decide future actions to implement.

A prime example that encompasses a set of multiple interpretations: an SME in B2B food supply - catering, amidst full digitalization in business development. Mid-year, the CEO calls for a plenary meeting where he starts talking alone while his entourage takes notes. Like in those pictures where a random Asian dictator points at a weapon of mass destruction, surrounded by engineers and physicists jotting down the Esteemed Leader's technical pointers. The key points were that his clients were too old for digital, that all new clients ordered significantly less in volume than long-time clients, and that the digital store was poorly designed because, in the end, almost no one bought despite spending a long time browsing the assortment.

While the Esteemed Leader spoke, I just listened and rummaged through Analytics for numbers that could confirm or deny these so-called certainties. Not for

nothing, but if it all had been true, we would have had to take some pretty radical decisions; if it was all false, a completely different plan would have been necessary.
At the end of the speech, I wondered how I could have even momentarily thought that the Chosen One's words were the fruit of any analysis.

Over 50% of the clients acquired that year (new clients who, moreover, now represented just under 50% of his total mid-range clients, given the natural demise of most old clients due to age) had registered a contact person under 40 years old. Under 50 was 80%. The remaining 20% didn't exceed 60 years: numbers that definitely don't scream, "our clients have family businesses where grandpa still makes decisions, and they can't use a computer." In short, the data said that this was a completely unfounded hypothesis, and that reality was quite different.

Moving to the average orders of clients, equating clusters (based on type, size, and location), new clients were producing an identical average cart (fluctuating by just a couple of euros). Not only that, this curiosity led me to an observation I would never have made if I hadn't needed to counter a baseless hypothesis: the progression of the average cart and order frequency over time (I had a few years of history available). It turned out that, equating clusters and across all client clusters, the average cart had been declining for years, along with monthly revenue per client, while paradoxically the average order frequency had gone from one every three weeks to one per week. My instant interpretation was that, simply, the market had changed over the years (a few years): logistics, digital, financial crisis, customs and habits, and who knows what other thousand variables had simply made more accessible and frequent the procurement of fresh Italian products abroad and at much lower costs. Given the ease of access, it no longer made sense for a restaurant to plan a month's orders and risk (given that over half of the order consisted of fresh goods) having to throw away at least a third of the merchandise, while it was more convenient to buy weekly only what was really needed, having to compete in a much more competitive market. I proposed, then, another approach: trying to provide a more "tailored" service to clients, suggesting what to buy to further reduce waste but sell more dishes generating more margin. A more consultative service, perhaps, from which to generate more revenue. I saw an opportunity in a fact (you can't correct the fact that clients change their ordering methods). My interpretation would have led to a course set by a series of actions and evaluation criteria, but I was told, in so many words, that I didn't understand a damn thing, so for the rest of the year we focused on finding clients who, in the same cluster, would order as they did ten years ago. Needless to say, how that ended.

Regarding the efficiency of the digital store, where little could be done except follow the Captain's indications which pointed to an abomination of practices totally opposite to the direction in which any e-commerce was heading at that moment, in reality, the numbers told a different story.

The average session on a very articulated e-commerce (many format variations, producers, and cuts, a lot of technical product information) was about five minutes, with just over 2,500 accesses per month (at the time, in the restaurant cluster, we had five hundred clients, half of whom were acquired digitally) and a conversion rate of about 20% and a jump of over 40% from adding to cart to transaction. Not only that: both conversion rates had almost doubled in the last year (indicating right decisions on improving the product). What should have been the goal? Why meddle with the platform with these performances (appreciable only based on one's history or at most compared to other sectors, which is inconclusive)? Needless to say, despite my resistance, we ended up working on a platform that pleased the Captain more than his clients, because "he thought it would convert better". We dedicated tons of hours to rebuilding that e-commerce from scratch, while almost stopping to look at automations that could lead clients to order better and more during their sessions. I don't know the result, as that was my last year at my agency, but I have no positive hypotheses about the outcome.

The problem is that this way of reasoning, this mistake that seems evident to everyone until they find themselves in it, I've also seen it in young, brilliant, and experienced innovators. Regularly, throughout the year, I see dozens of people relying on their taste and instinct and betting (even heavily) on their ideas rather than, much more simply, relying on data and their interpretation by team members.

3.4 WHERE AND HOW TO TRACK DATA

Most of the time, except in rare cases of high self-awareness in one's work and needing to juggle a million different data sources, you don't need much to collect and track data. A simple dashboard noting down the main metrics can do the entire job. And when I say "dashboard," generally there are two approaches:

a) The one who tells me, "Ah yes, we use Analytics." Well, no. The Analytics tracker is the tool that tracks data and puts it in Google's database. The Analytics front-end, however, is an analysis tool. Analytics should be used to investigate data, then those data should be used to calculate the business metrics you want to observe, and thoughtfully inserted into a tool (a dashboard) with a "diary" function, not for analysis.

b) The one who immediately imagines many colorful graphs and says, "Ah okay, so in these two weeks, we'll set up a complicated system on Data Studio where we cross-reference all sources and have all the metrics we need automatically and in real time, expressed in curves and pies." Well, again, no. Even in the worst-case scenario, barring the particular exceptions mentioned above, we are probably talking about a set of 20-30 metrics. At the very most, perhaps fifty. Metrics that, generally, change (in the way they are monitored) even on a biweekly basis. Building a complex system (which then won't work and will require more time to fix) for a small job is exactly the mental tilt of someone who plans in waterfall, representing with Gantt charts an enormous and articulated plan for where to go on vacation in August.

A CSV. A simple CSV. A very simple CSV, maybe on a very simple Google Sheets, so it can be accessed and manipulated by anyone involved with you. You can sit down with your team, choose all the metrics that seem important to monitor, and start calculating them over a period of history that seems significant to you. It's not "rocket science"; it's about selecting periods and copying (or calculating with a fixed formula derived from other already tracked metrics) the data into a cell. You can start with the basics (e.g., for an e-commerce, visitors → product view → add to cart → checkout → transactions), there's always time to add, modify, or delete them along various cycles.

	Inizio 24 Ott	Inizio 7 Nov	I
	SPRINT 5	SPRINT 6	S
MKTG/SALES			
sprint leads	12	18	
LEADS	381	399	
sprint trials	4	20	
TRIALS	87	107	
sprint accounts	1	13	
ACCOUNTS dati	12	25	
ACCOUNTS aperti	12	22	
sprint DEAD ACCOUNTS		3	
global dead accounts	0	3	
sprint 1st Orders	1	5	
CLIENTS	9	14	
DEAD CLIENTS			
ACTIVE CLIENTS (w/ 1st Order)	9	14	
%TRIAL 2 CLIENT	10.34%	13.08%	
%CHURN RATE (su client)		0.00%	
BUSINESS			
SALES	4	15	
#ORDINI PER CLIENTE	0.44	1.07	

The purpose of maintaining an updated dashboard is not just to have a colorful tool to show off when someone asks for numbers. The point is to have a common sheet, clear at a glance, showing the progression of results towards the objectives set by your team, making everyone "accountable." The numbers pin you down, forcing you to understand what's working and what's not, both in terms of the final goal and in comparison to the previous cycle. If in the previous cycle you had a conversion rate of 10% and in the current cycle you're not surpassing it despite having set a goal of reaching 25% by the end of the quarter, you are compelled to ask questions, reason, interpret, and try to figure out what actions to take to immediately correct the course.

3.5 METRICS: WHICH ONES TO CHOOSE AND HOW TO EVALUATE THEM

Numbers in themselves are not objective, which is why the metrics you decide to use should be chosen and treated as precisely and objectively as possible. In particular, your metrics should always be:

a) Objective: "A lot/little" is not a metric. "We had some downloads" is not a metric. The exact number of downloads in a specific timeframe, possibly anchored to other data points at different times, makes "number of downloads" an objective metric.

b) Comparable: You can't compare five apples to three pears. Among the myriad of abuses I've seen on small sets of metrics, the most frequent is falling into the trap of comparing different metrics. "Revenue has increased: we've billed about 50k€ since the project started, and this month we're billing 10k€." This statement only makes partial sense: technically, if I analyze monthly revenue, it makes sense to compare it only to the previous month's revenue, which in turn can be compared to the month before that, and so on. The same applies to the other classic example: "The CTR (Click Through Rate) was 3.5% before, now it's 2%, and indeed the CR has also dropped by 1%." CTR has nothing to do with CR, so they should never be compared or correlated.

c) Actionable: Every. Single. Metric. Must. Be. Actionable. If I decide to monitor a metric, I must be able to modify it. And by "modify," I mean that I must be able to take actions that directly affect (for better or worse) that metric. If I decide to monitor a CR, for example, the transition from cart to checkout on a site, by intervening on the cart page (providing more information to the user? Modifying the call to actions?), I can improve that specific CR. If there's no way in the world to control and modify it with actions, the metric you're thinking of should not be considered.

d) Measurable: If you can't measure it, it's not a metric. After all, if you stop giving yourself goals like "increase revenue" and start setting them in terms of "reaching an additional 30k in revenue this quarter," you can no longer use "a bit of downloads" or "the quality of my clients" as metrics.

Following this, there's the consideration of the metrics themselves. After choosing a metric that is objective, comparable, actionable, and measurable, you should constantly ask yourself: is it also useful? And if so, what is it useful for? An example of a metric that is objective, comparable, actionable, and measurable: the number of likes on your Facebook page. It's also easily manipulable:

just spend some money for an immediate return in the number of likes. However, unless there is a very close correlation between the number of page likes and your business goals (which can only happen if your job is PR rather than business development), it makes no sense to present or discuss it, let alone relate it to other metrics. In essence, it's not worth monitoring.
A prime example is the vanity metric of app downloads:

a) "We've had twenty thousand downloads to date." Who cares.

b) "In the last quarter, we increased the download rate from 1% to 2.5%." An indicative metric, although it depends on the goal.

Some reference business metrics to evaluate by product type.

In a two-sided marketplace (e.g., Airbnb, Ebay, Deliveroo), it would make sense to calculate and monitor:
- the CAC (Customer Acquisition Cost);
- the Supplier Acquisition Cost (how much does it cost you to acquire a homeowner or supplier who wants to sell on your marketplace, be it a restaurant or a store?);
- the number of matches between customer and supplier - if I have a hundred properties and a thousand active users, how many of these make a match and generate a transaction for me?

- the revenue generated from matches (along with the average revenue per match);
- the number of users needed for a match (e.g., knowing that "for every house put up for rent, I need on average fifty users to generate a match");
- the LtV (Lifetime Value) of each user. For example, a user who generates ten matches in a year for an average match of 50€ is worth 500€ a year;
- the retention rate of my clients (how many of them all produce more than one, two, or three matches?).

In a SaaS (Software as a Service, e.g., Spotify, Netflix, Dropbox), it might make sense to calculate and monitor:
- the CR (Conversion Rate) from visitor to free-trial;
- the conversion rate from started free-trials to actual paying clients;
- the Churn Rate (the rate of abandonment, i.e., the percentage of active clients who leave the service within a given time window);
- the Upselling Revenue generated by clients (how many can I sell higher-tier services to? How much revenue does it generate?);
- the MRR (Monthly Recurring Revenue, the revenue generated recurrently each month from my clients' subscriptions);
- the ARPU (Average Revenue Per User, the revenue generated on average by my users regardless of their status and type);

In an E-Commerce, the basic metrics to monitor are more or less always similar regardless of the sector:
-    the number of sales generated;
-    global CR on sales (broken down into CR from visitor to product view, from product to add to cart, from add to cart to start checkout, from start checkout to transaction);
-    Per Period Sales (number of sales generated in a given period);
-    Average Cart Value (the average value of each order);
-    Abandoned Checkout Rate (the rate of abandonment from add to cart to transaction);
-    the CAC;
-    the ARPU;

In addition to these basic metrics, it may make sense to monitor other more qualitative or business-specific metrics. In a company that digitally sells merchandise purchased from third parties or produced internally, it probably makes a lot of sense to also monitor the expenditure on materials for each order, the logistical expense on each shipment, and the margin after deducting these two and the direct marketing cost.

In all this, the concept that "numbers are just numbers" always remains valid. A CPC (Cost Per Click), for example, is a number. To define it as "high" or "low," a reference point is needed. And even having that reference point in a track record, it doesn't necessarily mean that work should be done (at a particular time) to change it. A typical example of CPC that I've often encountered is the case where the CPC is (let's say) "even" 3€, but the CAC is 30€ (a CR of 10%), and customers have an LtV of 300€. While it might make sense to work qualitatively at a certain time to further raise the CR to bring in more customers (based on the objective) with the same budget, it might not make much sense to try to force the CPC down (which, for example, risks leading to a decrease in acquisition volumes). A CPC is not "high because it's high," it must always be referred to the rest of the metrics being monitored and the objectives set. If the goal is, for example, to reach a hundred customers in a quarter with a given budget, working on the CPC only moves you away from the goal.

3.6 ACTION! (AND TESTING)

Every analysis and interpretation must (must) lead to action. Not making decisions and not implementing determined actions means leaving things to chance with fingers crossed. I often encounter the common belief that big decisions can't be made without extensive planning and production. The truth is, you don't even need a finished product to take measurements and understand the direction to head in. For instance, you can literally sell new features to test by "bluffing" (telling you have the feature, leading to the purchase, and only at the end revealing it's not ready yet) to track results and create further hypotheses to test. But, to do this, you need to move. In each cycle, the team should plan potential actions to take, and then choose what to actually execute, based on the analysis and interpretation of data from the previous cycle.

A correct approach to "actions" is "we need to increase our CR from 0.9% to 1.2%. What can we do?". At this point, the team has free rein to start thinking about a very short-term action plan. You can give coupons to new customers, find an additional offer to insert at checkout, shorten the checkout process by one step, or perhaps stop pre-registering users and let them buy (or try the trial) as "guests". The mix of actions that the team decides to approve and implement is the means by which a short-term goal is achieved, part of a medium-term objective, and based on data collected in the last attempt.

An example of the opposite? I recently came across an

early-stage startup where the CEO struggled to make important decisions. He saw the product as the only solution to problems and delayed any action plan until the product was functioning. While trying to at least define the main metrics and the acquisition model (the product was a sort of marketplace, so it was necessary to understand the cost of suppliers, users, and generating a match between the two) using existing tools and tricks, the CEO even paused work in anticipation of the product. The product was never completed, the startup was in a context where they had five total months to turn things around, and the five months ended without even understanding the numbers that could revolve around that business.

Post office employees stand still; entrepreneurs move. For a "cheat sheet" on how to move, it might be worth taking it step by step, number by number. And to do that, you need to decide every week what to do and do it.

Every marketing campaign, every sales session, is an experiment. An experiment, like in physics, begins with a goal, a criterion for evaluating the experiment itself (you need to be able to say when the experiment has gone well or not), and a series of actions contained within the experiment.
"If this UVP is wrong, with a new UVP we should see our CPC and CAC go down, and our global CR go up."

Early-stage startup, real estate marketplace. In an attempt to recover properties to offer to users without spending a fortune, and reiterating on the same UVP (based on the certainty of payment) for a month, we try to find another one to see if we can produce results closer to our goal. We decide to leverage a feature that doesn't actually exist in the product, but exists as a phenomenon: in most cases, our users don't need to visit the apartment to close a match. Same exact product, same description, only the UVP changes (so no additional work): volumes rise slightly, but there is a huge jump in CR and the consequent acquisition cost. The problem then became another: the volumes were still too low compared to those given by the objective, but it's a great example of how a test, executed on the basis of precise objectives and data, without any development, can bring different results and another perspective even using the exact same product.

4. IGNITION

Based on Scrum, Ignition follows defined two-week cycles (although this is not set in stone: you can shorten the cycles to a week or extend them to a month, depending on what suits you best and what you really need). Within each cycle, the same exact workflow is applied:
a) analysis;
b) interpretation;
c) action plan;
d) execution;

In essence, everything I've discussed in the previous chapters forms the basis for the operational approach to be applied to each cycle.

However, the framework includes a higher level of management, consisting of three steps:

a) setup and collection;
b) planning;
c) ignition;

The setup consists of the "installation" of all necessary tools (from trackers to dashboards to any tool you decide to use to assist in the process), and collection involves keeping the data recorded in a shared and easily readable location. It may seem strange, but not only the collection, even the setup, are moments that are repeated in preparation for each new cycle.

4.1 PLAN

The ignition plan, on the other hand, involves four interlinked sub-phases:

a) LONG-TERM BUSINESS GOALS: "long-term" can be anything that seems "long" to you. If the context is an enterprise, long-term could mean a year. If the context is a startup in an acceleration program, for example, long-term might simply be three to five months. Much has already been written about what a goal is and the approach to goals in this framework: long-term business goals should be ambitious and significant results, and the entire team should agree to engage in achieving them. Some long-term goals, for example, could be "by the end of the year we must reach €300K in MRR, over a thousand customers, decrease our

Churn Rate to 10%, and generate at least €50K in revenue from our new, yet untested product."

It may sound trivial, while in reality, this should be the basis of every action plan (business plan): I have realistic but ambitious goals, I must ask myself how to achieve them.

b) BUDGET DEFINITION: have you already allocated a budget to achieve the long-term goals? Recalculating, does it make sense? To be sure, instead of being guided by feelings, gut, and chance, it might be better to confront them with your track-record and goals. For example, if you have €50K to make a thousand customers, but acquiring a customer is costing you €200 and you have acquired ten in the last three months, it would mean reducing your CAC from €200 to €50 and, in the meantime, disproportionately increasing the volume of acquisition. It doesn't make sense. The budget should be calculated based on results achieved, compared with ambitious but realistic goals, and especially not conflict with each other (typically exponential growth and cost optimization go together as well as oil and water). Is it feasible? Decide with the team. Don't fool yourselves, stay grounded.

c) DEFINITION OF METRICS AND KPIs: which metrics do you need to "action"? Why? And how do you intend to do it? If, for example, the point is to produce a thousand orders, and given the budget, it means reducing the CAC from €30 to €7 in the first three months - a very difficult goal - perhaps it makes more sense to work on another macro-metric: revenue. The way to produce the forecasted revenue with fewer than the thousand sales of the goal is to increase the LtV of each new customer (e.g., from €150 to €250) and, perhaps, increase the return rate of customers from 10% to, let's say, 15%. This could allow you to slightly decrease the volume of sales while maintaining the revenue goal but having a bit more leeway: a figure around €15 CAC (instead of from €30 to €7) while respecting the defined budget.

Same goal, two completely different action plans, to be executed in very different ways, of which the second is realistic although complicated, but entrusted to the team's skill, while the first is almost unachievable and out of control, starting from improbable assumptions.

d) BREAK-DOWN OF THE PLAN: cut the long-term plan into a medium-term one. On an annual long-term basis, three months of medium-term can work. If the long-term is four months, a sensible medium-term, probably, is a month. All you have to do is adjust the objectives and KPIs to fit this shorter cycle. What do you need, at the end of the first quarter, to tell you that you are on the right path towards those thousand customers by the end of the year? Probably not a thousand customers divided by twelve months, because you will start from a slightly less optimistic history and will have to get the work rolling. So reduce the objectives, while keeping them above the data in the track-record. At the end of the medium-term cycle, together with the team, you will ask if the results are ok or not, you will look at the long-term plan with new pieces of the puzzle in hand, and you will be able to decide whether to change the long-term objectives or maintain them, planning a new medium-term plan with new "broken" and adapted objectives and KPIs. Likely, in the second medium-term plan, it will be time to start making the objectives of the cycle more in line with those of the long-term plan.

4.2 IGNITE!

It's time to burn cash (your budget) in the best possible way: not over an entire quarter, but in a two-week cycle. Less risk, more control: if you can't set and achieve short-term goals with a tiny part of the budget, why should you be able to achieve medium-term goals without changing something? The operational cycle consists of three phases that regulate the operational execution of marketing/sales actions.

a) IGNITION PLAN: This is the time when, together with the whole team, you organize the actions to be executed during the cycle. And when I say "the whole team," I mean exactly the whole team: marketing, sales, and anyone who plays a significant role within the cycle, including those in charge of product development. This happens on the first and last day of the cycle, no matter for how many hours, even if it's the entire day.

During the Ignition Plan, the team defines micro-goals that will help them reach the medium-term objectives. Based on these, the team plans actions to be undertaken in sales, marketing, and product development, each contributing towards achieving the goal.

An example? It may happen that you are not yet in a position to generate revenue from a new product still in development: the plan could be to acquire the first hundred users, online or offline, who begin to use the product in its beta version for free. This leads, in just two weeks, to having the first reference points on product use, which features work as expected, which are useless, which others need to be developed more quickly, and to the first measurement of key metrics: if a user using the product for free already costs more than the CAC planned, probably something is wrong and needs to be adjusted in the next cycle.

b) CHECKPOINT: Exactly a week later, in another control meeting, we ask ourselves: how are we burning the cash? Well or badly? Are we reaching the micro-goals we set during the Ignition Plan? This is the moment when the entire cohesive team must evaluate their performance and understand whether they will reach the goal or if adjustments are needed.

Alternatively, it may happen that the goals suddenly change: acquiring a hundred users in a free beta, perhaps, is proving physiologically impossible, in which case the team can decide to divide tasks differently (e.g., those in marketing can drop their goal and start providing more profiled users to those in sales), or to completely change the cycle's goal, for example, lowering the volume of users brought to service registration but setting a desired acquisition cost: in this case, the entire team's efforts must be dedicated to finding a way to onboard users more easily with the same budget.

The key question of the Checkpoint is: "how can we fix what we said to reach the goals we are far from?"

c) IGNITION REVIEW: This is the most fundamental and also the most critical moment for the entire team. We have always been conditioned to negatively evaluate failure, so not achieving goals can become the main cause of a poorly conducted review: team members, to not expose their weaknesses, will initially tend to "massage the numbers," providing explanations and justifications for their actions.

The reality is that the review is not meant to find a culprit for failure: failure is physiological, especially when the goal was ambitious. The team, at this moment, must be able to come out into the open and manage the failure as neutrally as possible.

During the review, in fact, you have to ask yourself: did we make it? If yes, the second cycle will be set up with the rhythms of the first and, in fact, with higher goals than anticipated. Because in any case, even when achieving goals, there is a physiological difference between the local optimum and the global optimum: the first goals of a cycle affect the long-term goals in an infinitely small percentage. Think you have a goal of a thousand new customers in a year and you've acquired ten - as planned in the cycle - in the first two weeks: the goal has been reached, but it does not guarantee anything in the long term. You will always encounter new obstacles and problems, you will miss many of the medium and even short-term goals, and after initial enthusiasm, you will tend to lose sight of the goal without understanding how it could have happened, bringing very high results in an initial phase and completely missing the targets in the long term.

For this reason, in case of success, in the next cycle, the bar should be raised compared to the general plan. One very representative reason for all: if the cycle's goal was to acquire fifty customers and seventy were acquired, and the goal of the second cycle would have been to acquire seventy-five, by raising the bar and bursting the goal, at worst (if you have worked hard to reach it, the goal) is to stay within the general plan without straying too far from the rhythms required by the long-term plan.

In case of failure compared to the cycle's goals, however, we must ask ourselves: what have we learned? What happened in reality compared to what we expected? Do we have new metrics we want to monitor or, perhaps, do we want to cut away some that, in light of the facts, have become useless?

But most importantly: should we lower the medium-term goals or do we want to insist? What goals, then, could we achieve in the next iteration?

The review is the basis for a new Ignition Plan, which should happen on the same day after a break from the review. The review is the moment we discover how we did, why, how to do better as a team, and give meaning to the money spent: having learned something new.

4.3 ENGAGEMENT FUNNEL

You're probably accustomed to thinking of a "funnel" in the most technical sense. For example, the funnel of an e-commerce:
- visitor;
- product view;
- add to cart;
- checkout;
- transactions;

However, you should get used to building your own funnel for yourselves. Two different salespeople can sell the same product by following different paths and storylines (different funnels with different actions at each stage). In the same exact way, the entire team should think: beyond technical funnels, there's no one precise and correct way to sell a product. Generally speaking, therefore, it's crucial to follow a macro-funnel on which to then build the actions to be executed during the cycle and experiment with different sales paths to the customer:

a) MOVEMENT: users need to be moved. Specifically, they need to be moved into your "machine". Regardless of what the technical funnel is (for example, the standard one of an e-commerce), the job of marketing (which will move campaigns across a mixed set of channels) and sales is to physically move a certain number of people onto the product;

b) CONNECTION: it doesn't matter what tool or technique the team members use, what's important is creating a connection with the user. Without connection, the newly moved user (for whom money has been spent to move) will not turn into a customer. Whether it's a landing page, a chatbot, an SMS/Email, a phone call, or a visit, the user needs to be squeezed (profiled) and stimulated to take further actions. Every time a user leaves a lead, the team should aim for a registration. With every registration, they should aim for a transaction. And so on. The user takes an action, we want a new additional action from them.

c) CLOSURE: the game doesn't stand up if there are no "closures". But the value of closures goes well beyond revenue. For every sale closed, the team should ask themselves if they are really learning who the "right" people are to move and how to connect perfectly with them, stimulating a second sale in a shorter time and gradually optimizing the cost. Closing sales without learning anything new means missing a step towards defining a stable and scalable commercial model.

4.4 USEFUL CONCEPTS FOR RATIONALIZING AN ITERATION

To better assess the results of a cycle's review, regardless of how the cycle went, some concepts can be helpful in rationalizing what has truly been produced and, above all, what really counts in evaluating your performance:

a) "If it's not a goal, it's useless." It often happens that, for example, the goal was to obtain, let's say, a hundred free-trials started with a budget of 300€. If the CPC (Cost Per Click) during the iteration was 2€ (generically considered poor by the person executing the task) but the cost of each new trial was still 3€, it still makes no sense to set a goal of optimizing the CPC by lowering it. I once dealt with a junior resource from a startup in acceleration: coming from affiliate marketing, a world where there are not many variables other than the cost of acquisition and the revenue generated (thus the margin you pocket), and therefore, by definition, optimizing all the cost variables of a campaign is the main and only goal of the job. Within his operations, then, the junior sought to improve "upstream" performance in each cycle, with often bizarre techniques, never looking at the business goal of the enterprise. Trying to optimize costs, however, resulted in an outcome opposite to the startup's objectives: with the same expenditure, even though he actually managed to decrease the cost, for two entire cycles the only goal (volume of acquisition, set in terms of a hundred free-trials started in each cycle) was completely missed in favor of a lower acquisition cost, a goal never requested.

b) "If it happened, it's important." More than often, initial hypotheses collide with harsh reality and end up with nothing going as imagined or planned. For example, it may happen that users, within an iteration, didn't behave at all as initially imagined, and are interacting with the product in an unexpected way, or bringing to light objections that no one on the team had yet considered.

Or, conversely, more rarely, things may go too smoothly compared to what was anticipated. An example could be setting a CAC of 10€ and maintaining, at the end of the interaction, an average CAC of 5€.

In either case, if it happened, it's important to evaluate it: any positive or negative variation from the initial hypotheses cannot be ignored. Instead, it should be taken as a solid basis for estimating new hypotheses and changing the plan: both for the following iteration and, if necessary, for the medium or even long-term plan (depending on the phase you are in).

A lower CAC, for example, instead of being a positive signal could be a symptom of an audience volume problem (and therefore could foresee a future "cap" of volumes, or the need to face much higher costs in the medium term).

c) "Keep the backlog updated." Every single day, if the team is facing new challenges without ever "sitting down", new potential hypotheses or ideas come up. Building a "technical" backlog containing everything that has been learned and the new ideas allows the team to have immediately available concrete ideas (for example, "automating a follow-up email in a three-step sequence" to bring to the table in the planning phase of a subsequent iteration.

Similarly, keeping track of everything learned about the customer or engagement methods allows for more efficient iteration planning. Knowing, for example, that customers buy our product based on their weekly budget and that the price is not important to them, while it's more important to take home more goods than usual for the same budget spent, allows you to act directly on both the volume of individual sales, the conversion rate of new customers, and, hypothetically, the same revenue generated (trying, for example, to upsell the customer with a strong discount on a particular product that he perceives as high value).

4.5 DO NOT DEPEND ON THE PLAN

The principles of the methodologies underlying Ignition (Lean Startup, Scrum, and OKRs), applicable not so much to daily operations but in conditions of uncertainty when aiming to achieve very ambitious goals without having reference points that clearly indicate how to do so, all have a common foundation: the condition of not having a plan.

Similarly, Ignition is not a methodology for better planning work: it is a framework that should aid in defining objectives and achieving them through experience. Given long, medium, and short-term objectives, no team should depend on a plan, nor should they plan concrete actions beyond the visible horizon (the "fire" cycle). Several cycles have led to the medium-term deadline: at this point, a new iteration should start for a second medium-term cycle and its operational sub-cycles, with all due reflections reapplied again and again. How did we do: good or bad? How are we doing compared to long-term objectives? Should we modify our objectives or should we change the way to reach them? What can we invent to make it? Is it feasible?

If the answers are positive, go ahead: persist on the same path and raise the bar in the second medium-term iteration. If the answers are negative, it's time to modify, even radically if necessary, the long-term objectives and the initial assumptions made to achieve them.

Who said that phrase? "Insanity is doing the same thing over and over again and expecting different results." Exactly. If you've come this far, probably the "we've always done it this way, and more or less we've always got it right" has stopped bearing good fruits. The goal of this framework is to give you a new perspective and a new context in which to operate, with tools and perspectives suitable for the times we live in.

Which incidentally:
"O tempora,
o mores."

GLOSSARY

- ARPU: Average Revenue Per User
- B2B: Business to Business
- B2C: Business to Consumer
- CAC: Customer Acquisition Cost
- CPC: Cost Per Click
- CPM: Cost Per 1000 (M) impressions
- CPL: Cost Per Lead
- CPA: Cost Per Action
- CR: Conversion Rate
- DEM: Direct Email Marketing
- MRR: Monthly Recurring Revenue
- KPIs: Key Performance Indicators
- LtV: Lifetime Value
- OKRs: Objectives and Key Results
- SaaS: Software as a Service
- UVP: Unique Value Proposition

AUTHOR INFORMATION

I was born in Valmarecchia, a hilly area in the province of Rimini, but I've practically always lived in Milan. At nineteen, I gave three years of my life to UPS, where I learned most of the things I still know about work. Meanwhile, I studied Communication Sciences at Bicocca, while, having quit my first job, I worked as a freelance web designer and sought my path by creating micro-businesses that could bring me money with what I knew and enjoyed doing.

I opened Vanilla, my digital agency, in 2007. Initially with three partners in an improvised office in the under-stair space of my parents' house. We went from digital marketing (when it was just starting to be talked about) to product development, working with both well-known and lesser-known clients on a lot of projects that gave me a very broad view of the companies out there, from startups to corporations.

In 2014, I also opened a coworking space, where I had the opportunity to come into contact with the startup world, which initially seemed distant to me, and I began to experiment by applying techniques and methods learned in my work, hosting events, and following startups in the ideation phase. I then started working with increasingly advanced and better-funded startups, and in 2017, I sold the agency to completely change my job.

Today, I am an advisor for digital business development: I resell the 360° experience I gained in digital over more than ten long and intense years, and I work mainly with startups. Sometimes directly, more often as an advisor on behalf of acceleration programs or VCs.

You can find me on LinkedIn:
https://www.linkedin.com/in/angelocasagrande/